The Comedy of War

Understanding Military Policy and Politics for the Twenty-first Century

Earnest N. Bracey

UNIVERSITY PRESS OF AMERICA,® INC.
Lanham • Boulder • New York • Toronto • Oxford

4501 Forbes Boulevard
Suite 200
Lanham, Maryland 20706
UPA Acquisitions Department (301) 459-3366

PO Box 317
Oxford
OX2 9RU, UK

Printed in the United States of America
British Library Cataloging in Publication Information Available

Library of Congress Control Number: 2006927295
ISBN-13: 978-0-7618-3538-7 (paperback : alk. paper)
ISBN-10: 0-7618-3538-5 (paperback : alk. paper)

∞™ The paper used in this publication meets the minimum requirements of American National Standard for Information Sciences—Permanence of Paper for Printed Library Materials, ANSI Z39.48—1984

To my best friend—Major General Robert Crear

Contents

Preface vii

I Introduction: The Politics of Military Pragmatism in Peace and War 1

II Of Ants and Men: The Failure of Military Politics and the Art of War In Dream Works Pictures' ANTZ 11

III Demystifying Total War in Disney/Pixar's A Bug's Life: Clausewitz and the Role of Civilian and Military Leaders 27

IV The Bugs of War: The Limitation of Warfare and Total War 43

V Implications of the Cold War between the Yooks and Zooks In Dr. Seuss' The Butter Battle Book 59

Afterword 71

Bibliography 77

Index 81

About the Author 95

Preface

This short book about military strategy and war has been a difficult undertaking, especially after the events of 9/11, and the destruction of the World Trade Center in New York City. It merged from my interests in how animated featured films and children books can explain American contemporary and popular culture, especially as such works relate to military policy, or the hidden political messages of war. It is original in the sense that no one has used such an approach (that I know of), in discussing war or peace. Chapter four was specifically composed for inclusion in this volume. It was begun as a way to explain war and military strategy and tactics, but it is far from complete. War is nothing new; but engaging in some military conflicts are still a mystery. Unfortunately, war happens far too often in human history. Moreover, the techniques, mechanics, and mechanisms of war are ever changing. And this destructive endeavor of mankind will be continuously written about in the future.

Toward this end, and equally important, we must recognize that, "A new interest in learning about war, [as well as] about matters that had been ignored but that now [dominate] public life, even an interest in gaining some kind of historical perspective . . . on the military elements [of] conflict, might be expected."[1] This book, therefore, is intended to contribute to the "on-going" discussion of modern-day warfare. It is also a way of systematically understanding what goes on before, during, and after war. War is a curious, but deadly phenomenon, manifested sometimes by greed, selfishness, or the unbridled ambition and avarice of humans. Furthermore, war is a military contrivance of devastating evil and violence, usually on a grand scale, with the common denominator or final objective being to win, to outclass, as well as defeat the enemy, and succeed at all cost. According to Professor of International Relations at the University of Oxford, Hedley Bull:

> War is a manifestation of disorder in international society, bringing with it the threat of breakdown of international society itself into a state of pure enmity or war of all against all. The society of states, accordingly, is concerned to limit and contain war, to keep it within the bounds of rules laid down by international society itself. On the other hand, war—as an instrument of state policy and a basic determinant of the shape of the international system—is a means which international society itself feels a need to exploit so as to achieve its own purposes.[2]

Obviously, what Professor Bull perhaps means is: War is extricably intertwined with our need to analyze or know why and how humans or nations wage war in the first place. What shouldn't be forgotten is, war is no small feat, as we shall see in detail in the body of this work. Additionally, this study tries to make us think critically of the political and strategic implications of warfare, and what's important and necessary when nations plan and engage in war.

In many ways, this study has been a pleasure to write for it contains or offers significant information about the military and armies that might allow national leaders to question their motives regarding the necessity for war. Further, this book tries to reflect upon some of the main political issues military theorists and strategists often look at today. In attempting to examine why humans engage in or wage war, I have included—as a former army officer—my knowledge of military tactics as discussed by two great historical military theorists and tacticians: The great Chinese General Sun Tzu and Prussian general and writer on military strategy, Carl Von Clausewitz. According to Professor of Political Science, Stephen Cimbala, Clausewitz succeeded in "anticipating the crux of the problem[s] in military preparedness or in war waging: the difference between making war subordinate to "policy" and allowing war to be submerged in "politics," in present-day terminology."[3]

We must, therefore, earnestly recognize the explicit and implicit burdens and responsibilities of civilian leaders when it comes to war—such as who will make the ultimate decision to fight? Indeed, should all the people of a nation be involved in making war-fighting decisions? Many times civilian leaders do not always take their cues from the citizens of a nation when it comes to war. Consequently, it is not the nation as a whole that determines whether the people engage in war, but it is actually the political leaders or civilian representatives who make such decisions. In some respects, nations that engage in war, at any level, pay a terrible price for their complicity or involvement. This is to say, some military campaigns or engagements might be antithetical to the health of a nation.

Interestingly, an equally important corollary to a call-to-arms (or war) by amateurs or inexperience civilian leaders is that they can undermine and disrupt a whole nation by their own personal, suffocating agendas, self-centeredness, and the mistakes they might make in directing military leaders. In this sense, we must remember that sometimes "armies [fight] on behalf of politically feckless purposes, or militaries [usurp] political power and [militarize] the state and its policies."[4] And such behavior can eventually destroy a nation from within.

Furthermore, as Sun Tzu in his famous military treatise, The Art Of War, believed wholeheartedly, it is "the unemotional, reserved, calm, detached warrior who wins [in war], not the hot-head [leader] seeking vengeance and not the ambitious seeker of fortune."[5] Nor should military and civilian leaders be brash, connoisseurs of blood and gore, or fight unnecessarily, and for no good reason. War is not a harmless endeavor. And taking human lives during such violent events should never be downplayed. Unfortunately, however, circumstances sometimes exist when war is absolutely necessary. For example, fighting for survival or national defense. There are some other important caveats in the matrix of war. In order to control certain conflicts or battles, one must also be a student of warfare, or learn from past wars, or the conduct of certain battles, in general. Indeed, as Professor Paret has written: "The phenomenon of war can be better understood by studying its past."[6] Today, even more than in the past, gaining knowledge about past wars are important and necessary in order to be successful on the modern-day battle-field.

More importantly, Sun Tzu postulated that: "the master warrior is likewise the one who knows the psychology and mechanics of conflict so intimately that every move of an opponent is seen through at once, and one who is able to act in precise accord with situations riding on their natural patterns with a minimum of effort will win."[7] Hence, the study of past conflicts (in a historical context) is appropriate because war, as we shall see, has ultimately "become more dangerous. And even the realm of the unthinkable—as theories of nuclear deterrence show—strategy and the need to study it have not disappeared."[8] This is why it is necessary for civilian and military leaders to defer war or opt for peace—that is, instead of direct confrontation and human annihilation.

The impetus for writing this book has been to clarify some dilettantes' narrow and naive understanding and interpretations of the military mind-set. It also tries to demystify our warped way of thinking about important war issues or policies. My excitement and joy in once reading Dr. Seuss to my children, or watching his engaging animated films, as well as my familiarity with the armed forces, and The Art of War, may have also influenced what I have written in this book. However, the specific discussion of tactics, strategy, and military policy, I believe, are right on point. I recognize the limitations of this presentation because of its brevity; however, I believe my approach is unique and appropriate for the layman and serious students of military strategy and warfare.

Furthermore, I clearly understand that the complexity of the subject matter would be difficult, so I used the approach of relating war and military tactics to imaginary cartoon characters in their exaggerated, animated form. Some may consider this a joke, but the major themes of armed combat and conflict in this volume are very serious. Thus, each chapter deals with a war theme or some aspect of war. Some might find my approach preposterous and absurd, but I believe the introductory chapter about the causes of war, as well as the analysis of Dr. Seuss' book, The Butter Battle Book, and the two animated films of war, Antz and A Bug's Life, and the fourth chapter, which gives us an imagined war with sentient insects, will provide some value, or increase our level of knowledge about the shortcomings of fighting wars and understanding human warfare, in general.

Again, it may seem strange or bizarre to suggest or consider parallels between the imaginary warfare of cartoons, insects, and mankind, but it is appropriate for our purpose. This work, of course, depends upon an open mind. It seemed sensible to me to argue the theoretical accounts of Tzu Sun and Clausewitz by employing the animated films Antz and A Bug's Life. Indeed, some children's tales and cartoons can provide us with specific and important lessons "about the inner problems of human beings and of the right solutions to [our] predicaments . . . than from any other type of story,"[9] which includes our need for exploring the lessons, futility, and horrors of war. In addition, Dr. Seuss' The Butter Battle Book can give us insight into our possible demise, if we contemplate using weapons of mass destruction in war.

In terms of substance, this little book is a simplistic way of examining military warfare at the higher leadership level. It also tries to give some historical insights about the reasons for fighting wars and particularly ending wars, and the choices we make regarding these decisive matters. Toward this end, a substantive argument of war cannot be adequately discussed without a fundamental basis or way of employing the works of two military geniuses, Sun Tzu and Clausewitz.

I also believe that this study is highly instructive in showing how mankind can resolve many inherent or crucial problems when it comes to waging war, or starting wars, or studying past wars. Indeed, how can humans curtail their dominant and aggressive nature? Or can we stop military conflicts before they even began? Clearly, the prospect of continuous war on this planet is always a provocative thing to study. Therefore, the final intention of this book is to explicate yet another way of viewing war in terms of our life and death struggles as human beings. But all that really matters is that we humans save ourselves from violent immolation or self-destruction. And we must use any and all means or diplomatic techniques toward this end.

NOTES

1. Peter Paret, editor. Makers of Modern Strategy from Machiavelli to the Nuclear Age (Princeton, New Jersey: Princeton University Press, 1986), p. 4.
2. Hedley Bull. The Anarchical Society: A Study of Order in World Politics (New York: Columbia University Press, 1977), pp. 187–188.
3. Stephen J. Cimbala. The Politics of Warfare: The Great Powers in the Twentieth Century (University Park, Pennsylvania: The Pennsylvania State University Press, 1997), p. 206.
4. Cimbala, "The Politics of Warfare," p. 206.
5. Thomas Cleary, translator. Sun Tzu, The Art of War (Boston, Massachusetts: Shambhala Publications, Inc., 1988), p. 5.
6. Paret, "Makers of Modern Strategy," p. 8.
7. Thomas Cleary, "Sun Tzu, The Art of War," p. 3.
8. Paret, "Makers of Modern Strategy," p. 7.
9. Bruno Bettelheim. The Uses of Enchantment: The Meaning and Importance of Fairy Tales (New York: Vintage, 1989 edition), pp. 3–10.

Chapter I

Introduction: The Politics of Military Pragmatism in Peace and War

> The Soul of Battle is a "rare thing indeed that arises only when free men march unabashedly toward the heartland of their enemy in hopes of saving the doomed, when their vast armies are aimed at salvation and liberation, not conquest and enslavement. Only then does battle take on a spiritual dimension, one that defines a culture, teaches it what civic militarism is [and] how it is properly used.[1]
>
> —Victory Daris Hanson, *The Soul of Battle*

THE CAUSES OF WAR

As a former Army officer, with over twenty years of military service, I have always been fascinated with the reasons how and why humans fight, start wars (or engage in battle), and ultimately kill one another. Indeed, understanding the concept of war has always been a preoccupation with me, as well as with, I imagine, countless other students of warfare. *War*, as we shall see, is something we should *never* take lightly. But what if one believes that *war* is always the answer or an elixir to all the problems we face as humans? Certainly some nations stand to benefit from war, like the elimination of a brutal or evil dictator; but *war* is not in itself a solution or entirely a means to an end. Military historian Charles Messenger has it right when he states that wars "have been caused by dictatorships." He continues: "Not only are they [dictators] prepared to make their own peoples suffer [as with the ruthless insects and humanoid characters in this work] in their pursuit of power, but they have shown little hesitation in using force to achieve external objectives."[2]

Having such notions in mind, it seems humans have grown accustomed, in many ways, to war without using *reflective thinking* to recognize *exactly* the unintended consequences of why fighting is even necessary in the first place. Wars do not start automatically, or in a vacuum or by themselves. Sometimes, however, wars do start out fairly innocuously. Furthermore, it is *unrealistic* to think that wars can be carried out without fighting, combat, and death.

More importantly, the pressure for nations to fight in mortal combat seems to continue to escalates as humans progress technologically. As a consequence, nations raise sufficiently large armies and fierce technologies to destroy those they perceive as enemies. The late professor Bertrand De Jouvenel has written: "Neither the aggressor's will nor the needs of his victims suffice of themselves to explain the vastness of the resource[s] deployed in today's war. Rather the explanation must be sought in the controls, both spiritual and material, which modern governments have at their disposal."[3] Indeed, are we too concerned about finding new technological ways to kill, maim, and injure one another? This argument assumes that mankind should care about the human equation; or that humans have the great potential for doing evil things. To be sure, one must understand and "recognize that war never has been, and is not today, a unitary or even a wholly military phenomenon, but a compound of many elements, ranging from politics to technology to human emotions under extreme stress."[4]

Consequently, any attempt to glamorize or valorize war is wrong and self-destructive or self-defeating, especially in understanding how peace should be won. In other words, no one should get use to the idea of fighting and dying in battles or war. Professor of Economic History, Geoffrey Blainey in his brilliant work, *The Causes of War* writes:

> Enthusiasm for war, or weariness of war, [does] not have simple and predictable effects. War-weariness for instance [can] increase the chances of war and at other times increase the chances of peace. Nevertheless those changing attitudes and moods merit a niche in any theory of war and peace. The memory of recent wars affects the attitudes not only of leaders but of thousands without whose support no war can be fought.[5]

What Blainey is saying in the above passage is that nations and leaders must *never* be swept-up *only* in the euphoria and glory of battle and, especially in carrying out blindly their military orders or duties and responsibilities in war. This is important or significant in grasping because, contrary to popular conception, war is not glorious, nor should it be romanticized. Professor Blainey has also pointed out that "Any nation's decision to fight, or to cease fighting, is based on a picture of what that war or that peace will be like; and one of the many influences on that picture is the fluctuating and intensely-colored memory of past wars or past periods of peace."[6] According to such a perceptive argument, humans can ill-afford to ignore the lessons of past wars, because it might be to our detriment in the future if we do.

Analyzing past wars, however, has always been particularly difficult, because many military strategists and theorist *never* witness war up-close, or first hand. Therefore, the problem can be with their varied analyses, or what they write about war can be flawed. Furthermore, they might lack authenticity in their varied interpretations. This is to say, many might be able to converse on the political-military implications of war, but such individuals will remain *only* dilettantes when it comes to actually discussing real battles and warfare, because they perhaps never personally participated in war.

THE MYSTERY OF WAR

In so many words, *war* is the uglier part of human life and existence. As Professor Messenger has concluded, the world of today "is a much more uncertain one than that of 1900, although in some ways the clock has been turned back to reveal the very same potential causes of war as existed then."[7] And one thing is certain: *Wars* can be absolutely debilitating or devastating to entire nations in terms of growth, societal goals, economics, and politics. Mankind, therefore, must think critically before engaging in war and/or following those foolish leaders who will spell our doom, regardless of their ideas and where they might lead us. For instance, what exactly happens with civilian leadership during times of war? Should it (civilian leadership) be subordinate to the military? Or vice versa? Moreover, to what extent should civilians involve themselves on the battlefield and in war-planning? And should military leaders shape military policy in terms of war? These are timely questions that are addressed in this work. Professor of politics, Stephen J. Cimbala has written:

> Wars are political creatures. They are fought for political reasons, pushed forward with passions, and terminated with political rationales for victory and surrender. To say that wars are political is not to say that the politics attendant to war are always handled well. It is the exceptional statesman who comprehends the military art.[8]

Civilians who oversee the actions of a military must be nothing less than altruistic and heroic themselves, else they will never win the day with battle-hardened, experienced, or superior warriors. Diplomacy and political discourse, moreover, may appear to some a luxury or a supreme waste of time; however, such political activities are fundamental to war-fighting tactics and military strategy. Military politics, of course, are but reflections of the cultural and ideological views of a nation that is not attuned to the opposing nation's will. Put another way, as Professor Hedley Bull writes:

> War is organized violence carried on by political units against each other. Violence is not war unless it is carried out in the name of a political unit; what distinguishes killing in war from murder is its vicarious and official character, the symbolic responsibility of the unit whose agent the killer is. Equally, violence carried out in the name of a political unit is not war unless it is directed against another political unit.[9]

Furthermore, many students of strategy and warfare believe that war is a political act, a calculated sort of madness that takes hold of a nation's consciousness and will when political discourse fails. One might also ask: Is war political *sabotage* at best? As will be pointed out later in Chapter Three of this book, Clausewitz offers "more insight into the important relationship between war and state policy than any other modern [military] writer." Professor Cimbala goes on to write that "a dysfunctional relationship between war and politics could contribute to military defeat and to loss of the state."[10] One only has to consider what happened during *Iraqi Freedom*, the second war in Iraq to unseat Saddam Hussein, to verify or test the veracity of Clausewitz's assertion. Hussein learned this the hard way. And, I believe, it was an expensive lesson. Still, not all victims liberated in war fully appreciate the greater military power when wars end. In this way, the outcome in war, in many respects, remains a mystery.

Nevertheless, the viciousness and utter brutality of war must always be seriously contemplated. For generations humans have fought one another, for whatever reasons, with one war being more devastating and destructive than the next. But in my estimation, there can never be real dignity in war. More importantly, one might even ask: Is there dignity in even perfecting the craft or art of war? Furthermore, is it plausible that humans will continue to fight and destroy each other in naked, brutal warfare until our final annihilation or extinction? Or can humankind transcend their supposed need to fight wars?

This work, furthermore, tries to deepen our understanding of peace in terms of war—or what it will take to maintain or preserve peace. Specifically, humans must continue to debate and agitate, asking new questions before making the ultimate sacrifice. For example, can war settle other political issues? Further, what can we do to stop the tide of terrorism? Even before the tragic events of September 11, 2001, where the World Trade Center Buildings were destroyed by fanatics, *terrorism*, which "is a form of conflict [or war]" has become part of the fabric of life in many parts of the world other than the Middle East."[11] Indeed, how can mankind establish a sort of transcendence of the human will to eliminate our need or predisposition to make war?

Additionally, and speaking in general terms, shouldn't positive and purposeful behavior by humans be opted over war? In my own view, war is easier to engage in than peace. Therefore, criticisms of war tend to follow the same old ideological lines. Peace is more preferable than slaughtering humans. It is not an exaggeration then to say that war and suffering, as well as politics are inseparable. Or does war and politics truly make interesting bed fellows, so to speak?

A fundamental assumption of this work is that wars can (and should) be prevented and civilian and military leaders or serious statesmen must give these concepts and strategies their highest priority and attention. It is also my contention in this brief study to show how careful planning, execution of other options and military strategy are vital for preventing wars—or at least ending hostilities early, or lessening the severity of war. One must note, however, that until attitudes change among mankind, unfortunately, there will always be wars. Indeed, changing the psychological, war-time attitudes and mind-set of men and women should be of paramount importance to humans everywhere.

Although war has come under attack by many liberals who see such barbaric behavior as a cruel detriment to life, and contrary to human growth and development, as well as immoral, there will always be inevitable grumblings about war.

INSECTS AS WARRIORS

In this short study two successful, full-length, animated cartoon films about insects, *Antz* and *A Bug's Life*, are used to to explore and investigate, as well as explain the general concepts of war, military tactics and strategy as imparted by Sun Tzu and Carl von Clausewitz. In addition, this study focuses on the possibility of combat between insects and humans, which manifest itself in an unexpected and inscrutable, imaginary war. But unlike the imaginative brain-sucking, fire-spitting insects from a far and distant world called Klendathu, in Robert A. Heinlein's classic science fiction novel, *Star Ship Troopers*, the warring insects in this irreverent tale are from terrestrial earth, interacting with their hostile and particular environments. This chapter is a greatly exaggerated account of insects trying to take over the world, replacing humans as the dominant species, entitled, *The Bugs of War*.

Oddly, the whole idea of an *insect* war in the distant future is quite plausible. Which is to say, this tale is not completely unrealistic. Or is it? Furthermore, the idea of insects going to war with the human race is not a new or revolutionary concept, as insects have been able to adapt and survive our efforts to destroy or exterminate them throughout the ages—centuries, if not millennia. One can perhaps see this fight as a continuing battle or *war* in itself. And perhaps this is not surprising, given that insects are more numerous than humans on this planet, yet on a much smaller scale. Still, it might seem absurd that insects could take over or start a war with humans. For example, there is no evidence that insects are sentient.

In many respects, chapter four is reminiscent of H. G. Wells' controversial 1898 novel, *The War of the Worlds* in that his pseudo-science fictional horror story presents the possibility of extraterrestrial life from Mars devouring the human race. In other words, super intelligent, insect-like monsters and their war machines attack earth, seeing humans *only* as food. Indeed, H. G. Wells speculated that, "If creatures [of only brains and tentacles] from another planet needed food to survive and we [humans] were food, would it not make sense to kill [mankind]."[12] The insects in this chapter, however, metamorphosed into creatures capable of *real* feelings—as well as a knowledge of their existence.

This is a significant tale only because it allows us to ponder the possibility of fighting some other creatures on this planet besides humans. It isn't hard to imagine. Or is it? And even though in this chapter, the subordinate insects are hesitant and are plainly uncomfortable about *initiating* a war with the powerful and *cursed* humans, the ones (or insects) that take over the leadership, plan for war with gusto, mapping out their terrific and impossible military strategy.

War, of course, is a complex challenge for the insects in this semi-fictional story; but the possibility of such a conflict with insects (in almost every form) is all the more troubling because it is entirely conceivable as one will see in this chapter. Given this notion, the implications for understanding the future in terms of strategic warfare are tremendous. More fundamentally, one must recognize that some insects are predator-warriors, and like mankind, they can kill with amazing skill and surprising efficiency. Envision a world covered with such creatures. Insects, like ants, also have special tools (or technologies) and specific strategies that they use to survive by annihilating—and sometimes enslaving or eating their enemies. Humans have also created tools or destructive weapons which can destroy or eradicate life on this planet.

This chapter additionally asks the reader to not only stretch their imagination to see insects as fierce fighters; but it also ask us to go outside our proverbial closed-minded boundaries. Mankind should respect the perfect efficiency and organization of these amazing animals. Under specific circumstances, one can easily draw similarities or parallels to the behavior of insects and men in war. Insects fight sometimes, for example, to preserve their species, just like humans. Further, the tactical strategies employed by the insect world in this chapter are novel in that their existence doesn't necessarily depend on the existence of mankind. Indeed, the insects in this tale see humans only as their enemy. This is quite understandable given that mankind have been fighting on this planet almost since our inception or *sentience*. And we must consider that humans think *only* of insects as pests.

Moreover, many insects, like the ants in the animated film *Antz* are indeed social insects, just like in the sense that mankind is sociable. This work, then, is a way to understand the forces of nature, and the insect and human world around us. This work also tries to simplify our knowledge of the warrior's creed. Perhaps one of the most crippling problems that will face mankind and insects for the future, it seems, will always be *war*. In other words, the debate will go on. Indeed, no question during the insect war in this work is more pressing than: How can insects get rid of the decadent and debased humans once and for all?

And what might be the unintended consequences of the suggested internecine warfare between humans and insects? Even if insects were to accomplish such things as presented in this tale in the distant future, humans would probably never learn of it—that is, until it might be too late. In this context, insects might be the species that succeed humans. More importantly, what effects would *sentient* insects have on humanity? This is the terrifying premise of *The Bugs of War* in chapter four of this book.

The question of whether *Antz* and *A Bug's Life* are leading animated films of *war* also remains to be seen; but I believe they represent a metaphor of our popular culture in terms of debating military politics and war. Ironically, the creators of these two animated movies probably didn't set out to make them as a way of understanding *war*, but they are able to aptly accomplish this feat —or this very thing—with their imaginative crawling, talking and colorful insect characters. Even the more technical aspects of warfare are presented briefly in this work, such as tank warfare and aerial bombardment with aircraft? Let me explain this further.

Like the Trojan Horse of ancient Greece, the animated ants in *A Bug's Life* build a large, hollow-wooden and multicolored, leaf-covered bird to deceive, frighten and defeat a threatening (grasshopper) fighting horde, which they pilot from inside this craft, like the Greeks, who built their wooden horse to breach the city gates of Troy. This is what is meant by a creative or *innovative* army being able to shock and surprise an enemy. Humans, in this sense, ride to some battles today inside enormous metal tanks or fixed-wing aircraft, and therein lies the Greek analogy.

The military mind-set is also definitely reflected in both *Antz* and *A Bug's Life*. These imagined realms can not only advance our knowledge of military strategy and tactics, but they can also shape our military world. In fact, it is the military implications of these two films that make them so provocative and interesting. In some ways the examples and lessons of *Antz* and *A Bug's Life* raise questions about the appropriateness of the *Just* and *Unjust* War. However, this study will not dwell on such specific matters. Needless to say, *war* and politics can be framed along the lines of complexity and simplicity; and in confronting military policy, this work briefly and inevitably discusses diplomacy. Indeed, we cannot discuss warfare without understanding, as evident in both of these brilliant films, the political context or military dimensions of conflict and *war*.

Nevertheless, the most important aspect of this work is to provide a deeper knowledge of whether wars are reasonable and necessary. As such, Sun Tzu and Clausewitz's ability to impart *intrique* and *complexity* into an understanding of the nuances of warfare is satisfying and quite remarkable as one will learn in this work. This study also give us insight into how battles can be fought and won, as well as tell us how civilian and military leaders might be expected to use an army and to act during times of war and peace.

In writing about military tactics and strategies of warfare, one inevitably crosses a path of many complex dimensions. Some opponents, for example, believe that war in and of itself is negative. Consequently, much of what one should consider in this study has been influenced by what experienced people know, in specific details, about past battles and wars. Additionally, and equally important, as journalist Chris Hedges has written:

> The poison that is *war* does not free us from the ethics of responsibility. There are times when we must take this poison—just as a person with cancer accepts chemotherapy to live. We cannot succumb to despair. Force is and . . . always will be part of the human condition. There are times when the force wielded by one immoral faction must be countered by a faction that, while never moral, is perhaps less immoral.[13]

More importantly, as already mentioned, how can mankind in the modern world come to grips with the horror and violence of humans in terms of war? It is important to note that the protagonists of these two unique films, *Antz* and *A Bug's Life*, ultimately do battle with two unscrupulous, tyrannical insect leaders (or dictators?), while struggling against evil forces that would destroy their entire civilizations. Humans have also been known to fight against similar odds and such evil forces. It is no accident that these emblematic heroes in the form of animated ants stand up to evil in its most terrible and unadulterated form. For example, the ant heroes in both stories show enormous chivalry in defense of their respective colonies, or communities.

Simply put, the insect villains in these two animated films underestimated the degree to which their ant victims or heroes would fight back. Moreover, the ruthless insect tyrants, perhaps, never thought they could be defeated. As such, and in the end, the villains not only lose the battle and the war, but also their lives.

Even more important, these imaginary worlds offer us a glimpse of warfare from another group perspective. The films appeal to both children and adults; and the popularity of *Antz* and *A Bug's Life*, I believe, owes much to their military bent. Collectively they also tell us much about contemporary military culture and the strains of human life and warfare. In the process of future war, the moral is: *Humanity* will somehow find a way to prevail, no matter that humans engage in *war*. And insects, these crawly creatures, will also survive as a result of the human race's existence on this planet.

Antz and *A Bug's Life* are instructive for no other reason than they allow us to recognize our weaknesses and potential mistakes as humans when it comes to engaging in *any* war. Even more importantly, through the study of Sun Tzu and Clausewitz's important military treatises, one can also raise pertinent questions about how mankind should raise armies and conduct war if there are no other alternatives.

Finally, the last chapter in this work, which is an analysis of Dr. *Seuss' The Butter Battle Book*, explains how ludicrous it is to build weapons of mass destruction which could potentially lead to a cold war, and ultimately destroy our civilization and perhaps our entire world. Indeed, we must never forget the lessons of our *cold war* with (and eventual defeat of) the former Soviet Union, as it provides us with an opportunity to understand similar wars.

NOTES

1. Victor Davis Hanson. *The Soul of Battle: From Ancient Times to the Present Day: How Three Great Liberators Vanquished Tyranny* (New York: The Free Press, 1999), p. 5.
2. Charles Messenger. *The Century of Warfare: Worldwide Conflict From 1900 to Present Day* (Hammersmith, London: Harper Collins Publishers, 1995), p. 394.
3. Bertrand De Jouvenel. *On Power: The Natural History of Its Growth* (Indianapolis, IN: Liberty Fund, Inc., 1993), p. 5.
4. Peter Paret, editor. *Makers of Modern Strategy from Machiavelli to the Nuclear Age* (Princeton, New Jersey: Princeton University Press, 1986), p. 8.
5. Geoffrey Blainey. *The Causes of War* (New York: The Free Press, 1973), p. 9.
6. *Ibid.*
7. Messenger, "The Century of Warfare," p. 395.
8. Stephen J. Cimbala. *The Politics of Warfare: The Great Powers in the Twentieth Century* (University Park, Pennsylvania: The Pennsylvania State University Press, 1997), p. 2.

9. Hedley Bull. *The Anarchical Society: A Study of Order in World Politics* (New York: Columbia University Press, 1977), pp. 184–185.
10. Cimbala, "The Politics of Warfare," p. 205.
11. Messenger, "The Century of Warfare," p. 388.
12. H. G. Wells. *The War of the Worlds*, reprint. (New York: Aerie Books, LTD., 1898).
13. Chris Hedges. *War Is A Force That Gives Us Meaning* (New York: Public Affairs, 2002), p. 96.

Chapter II

Of Ants and Men: The Failure of Military Politics and the Art of War In DreamWorks Pictures' *ANTZ*

> The rush of battle is a potent and often lethal addiction, for war is a drug. . . . It dominates culture, distorts memory, corrupts language, and infects everything around it, even humor, which becomes preoccupied with the grim perversities of smut and death. Fundamental questions about the meaning, or meaninglessness, of our place on the planet are laid bare when we watch those around us sink to the lowest depths. War exposes the capacity for evil that lurks not far below the surface within all of us.[1]
>
> —Chris Hedges, *War: Is a Force that Gives Us Meaning*

THE BEGINNING OF A WAR

The 1998 movie ANTZ is a witty, satirical, and digitally animated fable about the conflicts of war, unrequited love, and the failure of politics in the world of imaginary ants. It also introduces us to a fascinating way of looking at or understanding two of the most successful creatures on the face of the planet—ants and mankind. ANTZ essentially captures our imagination, although this unique adventure story can be viewed as an exercise in adult reality concerning war. Journalists Jeff Giles and Corie Brown write that ANTZ, "with its Woody Allen sensibility and Marxist gags, [serve] up a surprisingly adult vision,"[2] especially regarding war. This is to say that ANTZ is surprisingly effective at portraying truths and the reality of human warfare. Furthermore, by using the famous military theorist, and Chinese general Sun Tzu's classic book, The Art of War, one can explore some practical and important political notions, as well as other noteworthy applications, especially from a strictly military point of view in this bizarre fantasy about imaginary ants.

It should never cease to amaze anyone that both men and ants deal with the harsh episodes of war, and even questions of politics in the context of their respective social arenas and varied environments. Sun Tzu's sophisticated treatise, of course, has had important historical influence on military tactics, defensive capabilities and the strategic practices of many human armies in the modern-day world. Senior army officer in the People's Liberation Army of China, General Tao Hanzhang has written that The Art of War "should be studied from the modern point of view, selecting the essence and discarding the irrelevancies, making the past serve the present in order to develop it."[3]

Humans, however, unlike the incredible animated ants in ANTZ, and insects in nature, have been able to employ sophisticated new technical machinery, or military technology, (such as aircraft carriers, nuclear-powered submarines, as well as missiles and smart bombs) to engage in war. But despite the introduction of these weapons of war, or unique fighting devices and technical advances, mankind's ability or propensity to engage in war has not declined or dissipated over time. Additionally, the convergence of modern technology in regards to politics or political geography has meant that mankind can conduct war with relative ease throughout most of the world's hot-spots. Toward this end, Chinese General Hanzhang writes that studying The Art of War "will greatly help military commanders [and civilian leaders] at all levels in directing a war, organizing battles, developing wisdom, and increasing [war-fighting] ability."[4]

The late and best-selling author James Clavell, of Shogun and Noble House fame, in a rather brief and truncated version of The Art of War suggested that the book be made "obligatory study for all our serving officers and men, as well as for all people in government and all high schools and universities in the free world."[5] Clavell punctuated this consideration of concern and his unique suggestion by also writing that if he "were a commander-in-chief or president or prime minister," he would go further by having:

> written into law that all officers, particularly all generals, take a yearly oral and written examination on [the] thirteen chapters [of The Art of War], the passing mark being 95 percent—[and] any general failing to achieve a pass to be automatically and summarily dismissed without appeal, and all other officers to have automatic demotion.[6]

Why is this harsh and poignant proposal by Clavell so important? It is of the upmost concern, because war, one must note, is the result of failed politics, subterfuge, or corrupted political decisions, or the ultimate failure and breakdown of diplomacy. Even more significant, one must clearly understand that, no leader of a nation or "president should drag [a] nation into war without properly building public support for it. And no Congress [or governmental legislature] should fail to take a stand, yea or nay, on the issue" for engaging in war.[7] According to military historian Bevin Alexander, a great war-leader is:

> one who understands the changes under way that are affecting how war is conducted. This has not been a common accomplishment of military leaders. Over the ages, commanders have most often failed to perceive the transformations of war, and both soldiers and civilians have suffered greatly because of their blindness.[8]

Hopefully, future civilian policy-makers and military leaders will be cured of this blindness if they should be required to read Sun Tzu's The Art of War. We should also seriously consider that these decision-makers be required, as already mentioned, to pass a comprehensive test of the material contained in it. In this way, civilian leaders and military warriors will be able to do the appropriate or right thing when involving a nation in any future war. In addition, such a thorough military strategy or policy is bound to win battles and wars—that is, if we are to believe in the wisdom and sage advice outlined in The Art of War. Writes Sun Tzu:

> Victory is the main object in war. If this is long delayed, weapons are blunted and morale depressed. When [armies] attack cities, their strength will be exhausted. . . . When the army engages in protracted campaigns the state will not suffice. . . . When your weapons are dulled and ardor damped, your strength exhausted and treasure spent, neighboring rulers will take advantage of your distress to act. And even though you have wise counselors, none will be able to lay good plans for the future.[9]

Equally important and what many prime ministers, presidents and other high-ranking military leaders today have perhaps forgotten is: "supreme [military] excellence [should] consist in breaking the enemy's resistance without fighting."[10] But when war is necessary, it must be quick, decisive, and conducted without hesitation. Accordingly, an army must—as Bevin Alexander has written—"press straight into an enemy's vitals, and destroy the means by which he can resist."[11]

Warfare, or war-fighting is also superficially featured in the society of animated ANTZ, especially during their "Termites War" in this intrepid and impressive film. Militarily speaking, one must note that there is not much difference between men and ants when it comes to war and/or fighting for survival. Nonetheless, many in the ANTZ colony did not understand the true military implications of fighting the mighty termites and the significance or meaning of war. For instance, the deeply neurotic worker ant named Z (the voice of Woody Allen) struggled to know himself, as he is obsessed with profound questions of his own identity in that he wants to be something more than just a worker ant. In other words, the animated ant Z wants to get in touch with his "inner maggot," as he pointedly states in this popular and successful film. But Z is not initially a warrior.

Indeed, the ant name Z feels worse after being told that he is "insignificant" through specific therapy and analysis. Humans can also become depressed over war. But as the worker ant Z would find out during the "Termites War," and much as Sun Tzu pointed out in The Art of War, "When you know yourself, you are able to protect yourself."[12] The animated ant Z, of course, is one of the many ants who live in a unique ant community enterprise—a complex society of insects—that is divided on a functional basis of workers and soldiers. In this respect, ants in nature are very much like humans in their cosmopolitan society, which shows a vast degree of ergonomics and social organization.

However, the ANTZ colony is not an egalitarian society or culture. For example, in one of the opening scenes in the animated movie ANTZ, nesting in a remarkably beautiful system of colorful galleries and tunnels (a very large cave of sorts), white baby-ant larva are cared and tended to by nondescript adult ants. These decision-making ants unceremoniously identify the babies as either industrious worker-ants or soldier-ants. The smaller, worker-ants are mostly female in the film; but there are many worker males, like Z. The ants' ultimate objective is to excavate dirt, to enlarge the nest for the good of the ANTZ colony, as well as cater to the ant-Queen Mother in an autocratic insect system. It is not that complex. On the other hand, the larger-bodied ants are mostly males, whose primary responsibility is to fight to protect the colony. Worker-ants, however, in reality, as in this fictional ANTZ movie, control the food-stuff or the means of food production. Nonetheless, worker-ants can also become soldiers or warrior-ants like the ant named Z in this authoritative (ant-colony) structure—that is, if they are good enough.

ACTIONS BEFORE WAR

After the ant named Z convinces a friend and buddy, soldier-ant Weaver (the voice of Sylvester Stallone) to switch places with him for a day so that he might again see the beautiful Princess Bala (the voice of Sharon Stone), he is forced into an "unjust war" by a heartless, manipulative and ruthless ant-General called Mandible (the voice of Gene Hackman). And clearly, Mandible's militarism is underscored by what one might think of human generals and large armies.

Furthermore, this amazing tale of life, war and death in ANTZ is a story of love, because as the film progresses, the ant named Z becomes a war hero and later, a revolutionary leader in the ANTZ colony. Moreover, the ant Z falls heads-over-hill with the beautiful ant-Princess Bala, and later woos and earns her heart. Their first meeting or contact comes in a funny (and hilarious) bar scene, where the animated ANTZ socialize and drink something called Aphid Beer after a hard day's work. Indeed, Aphids are stacked high in a large, orderly fashion, like actual kegs of beer. This hip comic routine, of course, only adds a visual dimension to this war adventure story.

The little misfit ant named Z is then seen complaining about drinking from the posteriors of these pear-shaped Aphids. Many would perhaps say that this scene in ANTZ is like foraging ants in nature in that it is their "shortest path to food."[13] Moreover, this view is the ANTZ's way of depicting how real ants actually milk Aphids, because "the honeydew they produce is manna to ants."[14] As humans have a sort of symbiotic relationship with domestic cattle and other animals, the Aphids in ANTZ also have a relationship with the animated ants. For protection, the ants guard and shelter the Aphids (in this case behind the ant bar) for making this special food for them, the sweet, honeydew substance (a sort of delicious waste bi-product of partially digested plant sap), copiously secreted from their tails. The ant Z's exaggerated sense of self-importance is quite apparent at this farcical juncture in the film.

Also at this particular gathering, the ant named Z and Princes Bala dance an unrehearsed and spontaneous dance for the first time upon their chance meeting—which is totally against the norm and without the requisite ANTZ uniformity. The ant Z is smitten with the lovely ant Bala, even though he learns that she is the princess of the entire ant colony and is engaged to be married to the mentally unbalanced ant-General Mandible. Princess Bala is, in essence, a fecundated queen, or egg-laying female, who will one day start her own colony after leaving, perhaps, the original and prodigious ANTZ colony in a mating flight, as she is betrothed to the dreaded ant-General Mandible.

Additionally, and unbeknownst to the entire colony, the conniving ant-General Mandible thinks that the workers of the original ant colony are particularly pathetic and weak, a blight on all ants everywhere. Therefore, by mating with ant-Princess Bala, and quietly terminating (or exterminating) the weak-link of the first colony, by sending soldier-ants, loyal to the ant-Queen Mother, to an "unjust" and unwinnable war (and perhaps to their deaths), the callous ant-General Mandible tries to put his perverse military-political plans into action. In so doing, Mandible's unbridled hatred of his own kind is unparalleled.

Essentially, ant-General Mandible wants to annihilate the ANTZ colony and those ants he feels unworthy. This is to say, Mandible wants to put his evil plot and political objectives into action, despite the Queen's sincere reservation about him. Indeed, the ant-Queen Mother, as supreme leader, is distraught, as she is justifiably concerned with matters of state and insect governance. Furthermore, she seriously doubts ant-General Mandible's ability to single-handedly lead the ANTZ colony under her authority. In fact, the ant-Queen Mother didn't approve of the (dominating) way Mandible ran things. In this fable ANTZ story, the ant-General Mandible basically rules the colony indirectly. However, the worker-ants are not necessarily militaristic. General Mandible smugly reminds the ant-Queen that only he insures the fate of the ant colony. Similarly, Sun Tzu wrote:

> The strength or weakness of a country depends on its generals. If the generals help the leadership and are thoroughly capable, then the country will be strong. If the generals do not help the [civilian] leadership, and harbor duplicity in their hearts, then the country [as in the ANTZ colony] will be weak. Therefore it is imperative to be careful in choosing people for positions of responsibility.[15]

Perhaps General Mandible would have ignored the ant-Queen Mother's military advice anyway. But ignoring the state leader about the affairs of war is sometimes necessary. Sun Tzu, for example, was known for ignoring, when appropriate, the wishes of royalty, or civilian leaders—especially concerning military matters, or when he thought the heads of state were wrong. In other words, "Sun Tzu believed that the [particular] state should make up the strategy of war, and the commander should make up the strategy of war, and the commander should organize and direct the battles,"[16] without interference from civilian leaders or heads of state. But most important, as Sun Tzu appropriately points out in The Art of War:

> There are three ways in which a civil leadership causes the military trouble. When a civil leadership unaware of the facts tell its armies to advance when it should not, or tells its armies to retreat when it should not; this is called tying up the armies. When the civil leadership is ignorant of military affairs but shares equally in the government of the armies, the soldiers get confused. When the civil leadership is ignorant of military maneuvers but shares equally in the command of the armies, the soldiers [are] hesitant, [and] trouble comes. . . . This is called taking away victory by deranging the military.[17]

One must ask another pertinent question concerning civilian/military leadership: Should civilian leaders, state chairmen, prime ministers or presidents of sovereign nations, untested personally in the "art of war' and battle, be able to employ or deploy military forces and weapons during times of war? Indeed, how can such leaders cope with the major challenges of any war?

As the story-line in this live-action movie ANTZ continues to unfold, the ant named Z knows he must see Princess Bala once again—to somehow make her fall in love with him—before he goes off to war. It's a familiar, human story. Thus, we find our hero Z, after reluctantly becoming a soldier-ant himself, marching off to war in a "pass and review ceremony," or farewell-sending-off parade. The ant named Z, however, only catches a glimpse of Princess Bala, as he shouts her name, but is unrecognized from his minuscule place in the horde of other soldier-ants that finally stand at attention for the final encouraging words from the ant-Queen Mother, and detestable ant-General Mandible.

At this point, on the extravagant viewing platform, ant-General Mandible, in full, battle-dress regalia, addresses the soldier-ants, like George C. Scott (in the opening scene of the movie Patton), stating that he is personally proud to send them to battle. Of course, this fast-paced film clearly shows ant-General Mandible's lack of bravery or mercy. The ant Z critically views the whole scene with the ant-General Mandible as surreal and unexpected; and the idea of fighting the unknown termites terrifies him to no end. The animated ant Z wonders what he has gotten himself into. The animated ant Z also quietly ponders. But war is officially declared, with the grudging approval of the ant-Queen Mother—that is, after General Mandible convinces her (lies) that the termites are the actual aggressors. Of course, General Mandible's only intention or motivation is to compel the termites to do his evil bidding—to effectively obliterate the soldier ANTZ of the colony.

Essentially, the use of all the soldier ants—as instruments of war—becomes his [Mandible's] overwhelming and misguided military strategy. For example, General Mandible should have been concerned with his soldier-ant reserves, but he ignores this critical aspect of military planning, because it isn't vital to his evil and devious plan. Twenty-two centuries after Sun Tzu wrote The Art of War, Carl von Clausewitz believed, as did General Mandible that war is a "continuation of political intercourse by other means."[18] Pursuing an enemy in unknown territory, however, is not always good military strategy. But Mandible is not an accomplished or knowledgeable military strategist. Or so it seems. Otherwise, he would have known what Sun Tzu advocated:

> If you know the enemy and know yourself, you need not fear the result of a hundred battles. If you know yourself but not the enemy, for every victory gained you will also suffer a defeat. If you know neither the enemy nor yourself, you will succumb in every battle.[19]

Perhaps all civilian and military leaders of sovereign nations should learn Sun Tzu's insightful adage. Moreover, one should understand as Professor of Law, John Yoo writes: "In a complex world in which direct threats to . . . National security can arise without warning, a single executive [or civilian leader] can rapidly collect information, evaluate [war] situations and respond with force."[20] Equally importantly, one should also know the enemy before deploying such overwhelming forces. Furthermore, if Professor Yoo is correct, the question that still remains is: Do we really need massive military force to achieve any of our strategic and military objectives in war? The answer is not obvious. However, Sun Tzu reasoned, "He will win who knows when to fight and when not to fight."[21]

General Mandible, of course, is not concerned with long-term victory—just as some of our political and military leaders, perhaps, are not concerned—because his ultimate aim is to commit or subject the ANTZ to animated genocide. Which is to say, General Mandible wants to completely destroy his fellow insects and create a new ant colony (after his own fashion), with his young fiancee, Princess Bala. In this sense, the ant colony in ANTZ is challenged by overwhelming, terrible odds. The only other ant-leader who understands or who has known from the start Mandible's despicable scheme to wipe-out the original ANTZ colony is the mysterious and winged-ant, Colonel Cutter (the voice of Christopher Walken), who initially gives unswerving and total loyalty to the ant-General Mandible. But Cutter ultimately rejects him in the end.

None of the ants, from the start—as with Colonel Cutter, the winged-ant—really understood the consequences of their actions in battle. In other words, no one can accurately foresee a particular catastrophic event during war, even if one plans for it. For example, does any president or civilian leader, calling the shots in war, so to speak, know what he is actually doing? After all, one must clearly understand that there is no luxury in war. Sun Tzu astutely advised that, "All men can see the individual tactics necessary to conquer, but almost no one can see the strategy out of which total victory is evolved."[22]

Hence, the ant-General Mandible did not have a legitimate military objective by attacking the unsuspecting army of termites. But his pseudo-military campaign is a fraud, or just one of the pieces to the puzzle of his terrible and larger political plans. Thus, the ant-General Mandible's own "unity of purpose" enables him to prosecute the war against fierce termites to a disastrous conclusion, which he greatly expects and desires. Mandible is, therefore, not inhibited to fight, knowing that he might fail, nor does he fear defeat. Nor does Mandible care about the inevitable risks involved. Consequently, Mandible feels nothing can deter him from his true destiny or rightful place as head of a newly envisioned ANTZ colony. In this sense, one must understand that men too have been fighting wars for the very same or similar ideas and reasons for centuries: Namely, for territory, land, or some desired commodity.

In a nutshell, the ant-General Mandible finds it necessary to deploy a large contingent (or concentration) of his soldier-ants to battle the innocent termites, without personally leading the "war machine" himself. Is he then a coward? Not necessarily. Remember Mandible's ultimate aim, as already mentioned, is to destroy the "weak-link" of the original ANTZ colony, and start anew. Therefore, the inept military campaign waged against the termites in the film ANTZ is doomed from the start. Again, this is clearly understood and even expected by General Mandible. Furthermore, Mandible doesn't even care that the ANTZ colony might have been vulnerable to some kind of counter-attack. Perhaps General Mandible is afraid of death, or to command ANTZ troops in battle? Moreover, despite the dearth of knowledge that the treacherous Mandible has about the supposedly vicious army of termites, he still allows his fellow soldier-ants to sacrifice themselves. Finally, General Mandible is less forgiving toward his original ANTZ colony, as he wants to disassociate himself completely from them, for no other reason than his vanity.

MILITARY CAMPAIGNS AND OPERATIONS

By this particular juncture in the film ANTZ, the animated ant named Z has befriended another intrepid soldier-ant named Barbados (the voice of Danny Glover) who has never questioned military orders (in the past), or even thought personally for himself in battle. Perhaps Barbados should have questioned his orders as all soldiers must sometimes do. Because in Barbados' dying breath, after fighting the humongous termites, he urges the ant Z, "Don't take orders all your life . . . think for yourself!" But army-ant Barbados, like the other wacky, animated soldier ants in this movie, follow ant-General Mandible's orders blindly, without question or complaint, even though his military strategy is "bankrupt" and not carefully planned in advance, and clearly doomed to fail. For most of the soldier-ants, however, it seems like war is the right thing to do, even purposeful. Yet their steadfast behavior or mission to fight the termites is not really clear. Sun Tzu makes the following and relevant observations:

> In battle . . . there are not more than two methods of attack—the direct and the indirect; yet these two in combination give rise to an endless series of maneuver. . . . In all fighting, the direct method may be used for joining battle, but indirect methods will be needed in order to secure victory.[23]

From a great distance, ant-General Mandible deploys his overwhelming ant forces to fight the supposed termite enemies in a sort of shock or frontal (direct) attack. Therefore, many of the soldier-ants figure that they can win if they attack the termites directly and en-masse. Indeed, they become crazed ants, killers scurrying in the direction of the termite mound—full force. However, their fighting directly is to no avail. Unfortunately, the indirect method of maneuvering and fighting is never considered or used by ant-General Mandible. In fact, this timely strategy is ignored. To say the least, things go awry with the animated ANTZ as they sometime do with men in war. In fact, and in due course, both the ants and termites are utterly destroyed, invariably fighting to their death. "The Termites War" is also a war of mobility, like most wars conducted by mankind on the modern battle field, in that there is a vast, almost military-like movement of soldier-ANTZ in this film. In this sense, and quite frankly, "mobility is one of the things that Sun Tzu stresses."[24] Sun Tzu correctly warns:

> Do not attack an enemy who has the high ground; do not go against an enemy that has his back to a hill; do not follow an enemy that feigns retreat; do not attack the enemy's finest; do not swallow the enemy's bait; do not obstruct an enemy returning home; in surrounding the enemy, leave him a way out; do not press an enemy that is cornered. This is the art of using troops.[25]

Nevertheless, the subsequent mistakes made by the soldier-ants during the battle against the powerful termites is a classic example of not employing troops strategically or correctly in war. The termites on their own turf, have their backs against the wall, so to speak, leaving them no way to escape, so the termites have to fight—that is, if they are to survive. According to Chinese General Tao Hanzhang, which may sound somewhat contradictory, Sun Tzu also reasoned "in favor of gaining the initiative by striking first, fighting a quick battle to force a quick decision and not protracting a war."[26] Even so, heads of state, prime ministers and "presidents, as commanders-in-chief [still] need short-term flexibility in use of military force."[27]

Furthermore, when the army of soldier-ANTZ first attacked the almost invincible, huge termite mounds of "strange splendor," the angry and agitated termites are fighting for the survival of their home world. Ants in nature, of course, are capable of the same kind of aggressive behavior. But, perhaps, Sun Tzu would have advised against such an attack by the ants in this movie, as he might have counseled the ant-General Mandible against fighting a larger force. This is so because such engagements often prove impractical and costly in terms of lives and resources, especially, as one relate to the animated ants' courageous fight with the enormous termites. Indeed, the soldier-termites, in this film, are awesome, with large, ferocious heads, short, worm-like bodies, and incredibly strong mandibles (or pincers) for cutting and chopping, for which they use in defense of their splendid termite colony, like in actual nature, against the invading and marauding soldier-ants.

Often mistakenly called "white ants" themselves, however, termites belong to a totally different order of insects called Arthropods. More specifically, termites are related to cockroaches. Equally important, these battle-hardened termites in ANTZ used a technological advancement—just like humans use biological warfare—or incendiary devices, to repel the invading armies of the soldier-ants in this clever story. Nevertheless, it must be understood that human designers of "real life weapons . . . haven't matched with technology the precision that nature has achieved through millions of years of trial—and error experimentation"[28]—that is, in regards to termites' biological warfare systems. Meaning, the termites responded in a predictable, robust way.

The animated ant-veteran Barbados, also before his death, warns the ant named Z that during their attack, they would have to watch out for the cleaver termites' squirting of a sticky and poisonous secretion from their heads—a chemical (insect) spray which they have no defense against. To also make matters even worse, this sort of incendiary weapon, an insect-based toxin, or chemical warfare, created in their bodies, is used by the termites as a type of "fire power" in ANTZ. And this is why the ant hero, named Z is extremely afraid. According to Sun Tzu, "the use of fire [or incendiary devices] must have a basis, and requires certain tools. There are appropriate times for setting fires, namely when the weather is dry and windy."[29] And the battle conditions are ideal for the use of fire or incendiary devices in this ant-war film. Indeed, the warring army of termites kill the ants with impunity with this insect technology.

In essence, and once provoked, the deadly termites in ANTZ employ five noted types of incendiary techniques in their attack against General Mandible's animated solder-ants. As Sun Tzu suggested in The Art of War, an army in battle must first try "to incinerate men [or ants, in our case], the second to incinerate provisions, the third to incinerate supply trains, the fourth to incinerate armories, and the fifth to incinerate formations."[30] In this sense, and as in the movie ANTZ, the fighting termites use certain strategies and tactics to win wars, employing defensive capabilities, just like humans.

Furthermore, the ant-soldiers in ANTZ hold their own, initially, in the "Termites War," which thereafter becomes increasingly brutal, total and destructive. Perhaps the animated soldier ants were not expecting such a capable and formidable termite fighting force. This is to say, and to paraphrase Sun Tzu, "A larger army can be defeated by a smaller one if the conditions are right." Equally significant, as Sun Tzu counseled, "If you are equal, then fight if you are able. If you are fewer, then keep away if you are able."[31] Clearly in battle and war, one must know when to fight, when not to fight, and when to retreat. Indeed, being at a disadvantage, the ant-soldiers in the film ANTZ are unable to flee, or retreat, so their attacking columns are eventually massacred. Moreover, the hard-fighting termites are ultimately destroyed at the end of the fighting, too. But fortunately, the ant named Z is able to survive his ordeal, or this war.

Sun Tzu succinctly wrote that "when the officers [like the ant-General Mandible, ant-Colonel Cutter and other selected soldier-ant leaders in ANTZ] are too strong and the common soldiers too weak, the result is collapse,"[32] as is the case in the soldier ants' awful and sound defeat by the proud and animated termites at the mounds of "strange splendor." However, ant-General Mandible achieves the political objectives he actually intended for conducting the "unjust" war in the first place. Hence, the total war campaign by General Mandible is waged not only against the battle-hardened termites, but also against part of the original ant colony—and their means of existence.

As already mentioned, General Mandible's only purpose is to destroy the means and will of his own kind for a new colony. Perhaps Mandible's "ethnic cleansing" philosophy, or depraved, "means-to-an-end" logic are reminiscent of other totalitarian leaders (and their military henchmen and cronies) who commit unspeakable and terrible atrocities; and where they eliminate those that don't acquiesce or fit the image or mold in their New World Orders.

And despite all of his strategic military mistakes and tactical errors, the ant-General Mandible survives the war by not physically participating himself—that is, he is never visible where the ANTZ troops can see him on the battlefield. Perhaps Mandible was trying to "mystify" his army of soldier ants by giving them "false reports," and not showing his wicked intentions, and "thus [keeping] them in total ignorance"[33] before they all died (that is, except the ant named Z). The ant-General Mandible, as well as many heads-of-state should take heed of Sun Tzu's pragmatic or practical words of advice, otherwise they too might put soldiers unnecessarily in harm's way. Indeed, if our "military and political leaders" had seriously studied The Art of War, as the late James Clavell suggested:

> Vietnam could not have happened; we would not have lost the war in Korea (we lost because we did not achieve victory); the Bay of Pigs could not have occurred; the hostage fiasco in Iran would not have come to pass . . . and, in all probability, World Wars I and II would have been avoided—certainly they would not have been waged as they were waged, and the millions of youths obliterated unnecessarily and stupidly by monsters calling themselves generals would have lived out their lives.[34]

The ant-General Mandible, like some men, could not control his vain, rapacious and murderous thoughts and actions; and this craven behavior becomes his undoing. To be sure, had ant-General Mandible survived in this wonderfully imaginative film ANTZ, he certainly should have been held accountable for his actions, or tried as a war criminal. Perhaps one must remember that all murderous and authoritarian dictators, pompous kings and tyrants will eventually receive their just desert or punishment for the lives they steal, or destroy.

CONCLUSIONS

Although a victory of sorts is finally attained or achieved by the little worker-soldier-ant Z, as he is the only one that makes it back home from the death-ridden battlefield of termites and ants, General Mandible, before his death, is terribly upset that someone—like a cursed worker, turned soldier-ant, might interfere with his glorious and future political plans to usurp authority from the ant-Queen Mother and form a new ANTZ colony.

Nevertheless, in a brilliant stroke of nerves and gumption, Mandible declares that the ant named Z is a "war hero," bringing him before the rest of the cheering crowd of colony ants, stating that Z, "Looked death in the face and laughed." This change of heart on the part of the ant General is important to understand, because as Hedges writes:

> We call on the warrior to exemplify the qualities necessary to prosecute war—courage, loyalty, and self-sacrifice. The soldier, neglected and even shunned during peacetime, is suddenly held up as the exemplar of our highest ideals, the savior of the state. The soldier is often whom we want to become, although secretly many of us, including most soldiers, know that we can never match the ideal held out before us.[35]

The ant named Z is absolutely amazed, or befuddled by the ant General's strange pronouncement. General Mandible is obviously jealous, but he makes it seem like the animated ant Z is an ant of his own heart, who always makes the best of things. Perhaps, in this sense, one can see that Z is a reluctant soldier-ant hero. But upon seeing the ant-Princess Bala again, the ant Z is carried away (to impress her) by the thrill of the moment, proclaiming and going alone enthusiastically that, "In the heat of battle . . . you must attack, attack!" Perhaps the ant named Z is familiar, intuitively, with Sun Tzu's The Art of War, because he tries hard not to reveal, or hide his anti-war aesthetics. After all, Z is now considered an army-ant-soldier-hero.

Meanwhile, when the animated ant Z finally greets Princess Bala again (with some familiarity), General Mandible sardonically eyes the ant Z. Moreover, with acute and murderous suspicion, Mandible immediately displays his disgust and anger upon learning that the ant named Z had the audacity to dance with his fiancee, Princess Bala, in a seedy Aphid Bar, as he believes she is still essential to his future plans for a new ANTZ colony. Hence, General Mandible turns on the ant Z for having the temerity of touching Bala; later proclaiming that the animated ant Z is now an enemy of the state (or ANTZ colony).

In the confusion and mayhem that ensues—that is, while General Mandible tries to apprehend him—Z takes Princess Bala hostage, fumbling away from the ANTZ palace with her in tow. The two insects are clearly angry with each other. And referring to General Mandible, the ant named Z asks Princess Bala incredulously, "Do you really want to be Mrs. Raving Lunatic?" On the other hand, Princess Bala is also amazed—perhaps impressed—that the meek ant Z had the temerity to pass himself off as a soldier-ant. In fact, Princess Bala explains that when she first entered the ant-colony Aphid Bar, she was looking for action, and selected the animated ant Z, because he was the most pathetic looking bug in the joint.

Later, their feelings for each other warmed as the two discover the mythical Insectopia (a sort of utopia), or the land of endless good food and edible garbage, together. But Princess Bala is eventually found and brought back forcibly and unceremoniously to the ANTZ colony by the winged-ant Colonel Cutter. At the same time, a spontaneous revolution of sorts takes place in the ANTZ colony, and the worker-ants rise up in the name of the worker-revolutionary ant Z—that is, upon his return from Insectopia. No longer would they be "Pawns of the Oppressive [ANTZ] State," many worker-ants angrily shout. Then many of them walk-off their dirt-excavating jobs, until ant-General Mandible—known for his eloquent and persuasive speeches—convinces them that the ant-revolutionary Z didn't really make a difference in their insect lives. And unfortunately, Mandible wins them over again.

General Mandible, moreover, is worried that the old ant colony's spate of individualism is becoming dangerous, and would undermine his master plan to complete a Mega-tunnel in which he would drown the remaining ANTZ colony members, save a few of his loyal followers and cohorts. Scrambling to save their colony from flooding and drowning, and Mandible's evil machinations, the ant named Z comes to the rescue by having the worker-ants quickly build a bridge of sorts, a chain of worker-ant bodies, which reached the surface of the Mega-tunnel. The ant Z's innovative thinking-on-his-feet foils the ant-General's wicked plot to destroy them. But in a desperate and last ditch effort to save his deceptive and terrible plan, Mandible lunges at the ant named Z, to swash him from the surface of their life-saving tunnel-opening, but instead, he plunges to his death.

Afterward, the intrepid ant colony is rebuilt, stronger and better, and the ant named Z gets the girl (Princess Bala), eventually having a few million ant-larva, or eggs to boot. And in the end, the ant named Z turns out to be the biggest hero of them all. ANTZ, a terse, sociological and philosophical adult film gives a new dimension to animated cartoons, combining social criticism about life, death, and war, as well as about military politics, and how, perhaps, The Art of War can be used to fight battles or other conflicts throughout the world. All in all, the great Sun Tzu propagated his wise ideas, espousing military and political propaganda that was against starting wars (for inappropriate reasons) by preventing the underlying reasons for waging war. One might again ask: How can humans in fact divest ourselves from perhaps the lunacy and horrors of war? The Art of War provides us with a definitive answer: By not starting wars in the first place. Therefore, this masterpiece on military strategy and tactics is a valuable message for our times.

Furthermore, Sun Tzu's important work tells us what can happen with careless generals or inept military and political leaders. Ultimately, The Art of War should be an integral part of any leader's study of war, especially for those who would undermine the process of peace. Lastly, one must ask: Can civilian or military leaders really justify the introduction of troops anywhere in the world today without trying every means at our disposal for diplomacy? Shouldn't nations in fact be concerned with investing in peace and stopping wars everywhere in the world today? Indeed, how exactly might human beings accomplish such a worthwhile feat or endeavor? As pointed out by Sun Tzu, The Art of War's basic thesis is "to try to overcome the enemy by wisdom, not by force alone."[36] In the final analysis, one must understand that The Art of War "is of vital importance to the state. It is a matter of life and death, a road either to safety or to ruin. Hence under no circumstances can it be neglected,"[37] or ignored.

NOTES

1. Chris Hedges. War: Is A Force That Gives Us Meaning (New York: Public Affairs, 2002), p. 3
2. Jeff Giles and Corie Brown, "This Bug's For You," *Newsweek* (November 16, 1998), p. 79.
3. General Tao Hanzhang. Translated by Yuan Shibing. Sun-Tzu's Art of War: The Modern Chinese Interpretation (New York: Sterling Publishing Company, Inc., 1990), p. 8.
4. Ibid.
5. James Clavell, editor. Sun-Tzu. The Art of War (New York: Delacorte Press, 1983), p. 7.
6. Ibid.
7. "Today's debate: Making War," *USA Today* (May 25, 1999), p. 13A.
8. Bevin Alexander. How Wars Are Won: The 13 Rules of War—From Ancient Greece to the War on Terror (New York: Crown Publishers, 2002), p. 8.

9. Samuel B. Griffith, translator with an Introduction. Sun-Tzu. The Art of War (New York: Oxford University Press, 1963), pp. 72-73.
10. Clavell, "Sun-Tzu, The Art of War," p. 15.
11. Alexander, "How Wars Are Won," p. 180.
12. Thomas Clearly, translator. Sun-Tzu. The Illustrated Art of War (Boston, Massachusetts: Shambhala, 1998), p. 109.
13. Michael Crichton. Prey: A Novel (New York: Harper Collins, 2002), p. 10.
14. "Herbivorous ants: Veggie burgers, anyone?" The Economist (May 10, 2003), p. 70.
15. Clearly, "Sun-Tzu, The Illustrated Art of War," p. 103.
16. Tao Hanzhang, "Sun-Tzu's Art of War," p. 28.
17. Clearly, "sun-Tzu, The Illustrated Art of War," p. 104.
18. Michael Howard and Peter Paret, editors. Carl von Clausewitz. On War (Princeton, New Jersey: Princeton University Press), p. 87.
19. Clavell, "Sun-Tzu, The Art of War," p. 18.
20. John Yoo, "President Has Right to Initiate War," USA Today (May 25, 1999), p. 13A.
21. Clavell, "Sun-Tzu, The Art of War," p. 17.
22. Ibid., pp. 28-29.
23. Clavell, "Sun-Tzu, The Art of War," pp. 21-22.
24. Ibid., p. 6.
25. Roger T. Ames, translator, with an Introduction and Commentary. Sun-Tzu. The Art of Warfare: The First English Translation incorporating the recently discovered Yin-Ch'ueh-Shan Texts (New York: Ballantine Books, 1993), pp. 131-132.
26. Tao Hanzhang, "Sun-Tzu's Art of War: The Modern Chinese Interpretation," p. 28.
27. "Today's debate: Making War," p. 13A.
28. Tim Friend, "Captured on Film: A Bombardier Beetle With Wicked Aim," USA Today (August 17, 1999), p. 7P.
29. Clearly, "Sun-Tzu, The Illustrated Art of War," p. 215.
30. Ralph D. Sawyer, translator, with an Introduction and Commentary. Sun-Tzu. The Art of War (New York: Barnes and Noble, 1994), p. 227.
31. Clearly, "Sun-Tzu, The Illustrated Art of War," p. 100.
32. Clavell, "Sun-Tzu, The Art of War," p. 64.
33. Ibid., pp. 1-2.
34. Ibid.
35. Hedges, "War: Is A Force That Gives Us Meaning," p. 11.
36. Tao Hanzhang, "Sun-Tzu's Art of War: The Modern Chinese Interpretation," p. 13.
37. Clavell, "Sun-Tzu, The Art of War," p. 9.

Chapter III

Demystifying Total War in Disney/ Pixar's A Bug's Life: Clausewitz and the Role of Civilian and Military Leaders

> And in the end it was all, or nearly all, useful and necessary. Undeniably, there were immense confusions in the resultant production effort and there were mistakes and misdirections of effort in the military planning.[1]
>
> —Walter Millis,
> *Arms and Men: A Study of American Military History*

INTRODUCTION

From the outset, it must be clearly understood what the famous Prussian general and military author, Carl von Clausewitz meant when he wrote that war is "a continuation of political activity by other [violent] means."[2] This Clausewitzian maxim, of course, is widely understood and firmly grounded in perhaps the minds of many civilian leaders and military strategists today. Director and film-maker John Lasseter's animated 1994 movie, *A Bug's Life* also focuses on such Clausewitzian notions, especially in analyzing the fields of military policy and presenting the political implications of *war*. In other words, this animated film is also a metaphoric way of exploring things such as life, death, and war.

A Bug's Life centers on an animated ant with "a self-esteem problem,"[3] named Flik (the voice of Dave Foley), the main bug character, who becomes a military strategist and self-made warrior. Flik, of course, in the main body of the film, *A Bug's Life*, understood many of Clausewitz's concepts. Clausewitz, the great philosopher of war, believed that *violence* and *political impact* are two permanent characteristics of war,[4] and that the military establishment is an instrument of the state (or nations) and its civilian leadership.

The military is also a collective tool of force to be used in war or combat operations, if necessary, to carry out a government's national policy and military strategy objectives.

Military strategy, of course, is a nation's use of its armed forces or military to wage war on a massive or grand scale, primarily because of failed policies that arise from its involvement in state affairs, or what Clausewitz called the important "use of engagements for the object of war."[5] Military strategy is also that part of warfare that fringes on politics and diplomacy, or that territory (of war) where the military leader and statesmen [civilian leaders] focus, merge, or coalesce—and where it is "exclusively the province of generals and other senior officers."[6] Clausewitz succinctly explained:

> The first, the supreme, the most far-reaching act of judgment that the statesman and [military] commander have to make is to establish by that test the kind of war on which they are embarking: neither mistaking it for, nor trying to turn it into something that is alien to its nature. This is the first of all strategic questions and the most comprehensive.[7]

The purpose of this chapter, therefore, is not to survey a history of war or to discuss some specific foreign policy, or military strategy. There are numberous works already that discuss such matters. It is rather a brief discourse on the necessity of fighting wars, and to explain how Clausewitz has had, and continues to have, a profound influence on American military strategy. Additionally, it discusses how *war*, what Clausewitz called "a remarkable trinity,"[8] must be expediently or expeditiously waged, if such actions are to be successful, as in the feature film, *A Bug's Life*. The animated Flik clearly understood this "remarkable trinity" when he had the audacity to recruit "warrior-bugs" to help him fight for the survival of his ant colony against rampaging, voracious grasshopper terrorists.

This chapter also explains how the military leader and civilian statesman should *interact* and relate to enact policy in accordance with Clausewitzian philosophy. In this sense, the hapless ant Flik in this animated farce becomes both a diplomat and heroic warrior to fend off "a marauding [sort of] motorcycle gang of grasshoppers led by the evil Hopper (the voice of Kevin Spacey)."[9]

THE ROLE OF MILITARY LEADERS

The art of military command and the very foundation of a theory of warfare rests on the clear understanding, as we pointed out previously, that war is a continuation of politics, or policy,[10] or the result of neglected or unsuccessful diplomacy. Thus, if all other things are equal, we should be cognizant that "the personalities of [the civilian] statesman and [military] soldiers are such important factors that in war above all it is vital not to underrate them."[11] Clausewitz astutely and clearly inferred that: "To bring a war, or one of its campaigns, to a successful close [or end] requires a thorough grasp of national policy. On that level, strategy and policy coalesce: the commander-in-chief [or supreme military leader] is simultaneously a statesman."[12] This is to say that senior military leaders *cannot* abstain necessarily from participating in diplomatic matters and the formulation of related policy, nor "preparedness for war" considerations. It should be noted, moreover, that the military must *never* dictate policy in a democracy—that is, if that democracy is to survive.

The weirdly absorbed Flik in *A Bug's Life*, for example, consciously made a fundamental decision to fight the pesky grasshoppers. And Flik made a huge difference. The ant colony in this animated story was genuinely unhappy with their arrangement (to provide free food) to the dreaded grasshoppers. On the Island of the Animated Ants in this story, the colony congregated in a sort of multitude, existing in an insect world of their own choosing; and the grasshoppers were beyond contempt. The grasshoppers felt, without hesitation, that the ants' harvest was theirs to appropriate, to take. Flik, in preparing for war, sensed that his moment for glory and fame had at last arrived. But he came to believe it was his blind duty to go against the grain-eating grasshoppers.

Again, the animated ant colony in *A Bug's Life* had had their fill of the troublesome grasshoppers and their *anything*-goes-attitude was infectious. In either case, the nervous colony ants decided to exhaust their options by allowing the enthusiastic Flik to recruit "warrior bugs," perhaps against their better judgment to help them. And Flik's lonesome journey to the city (where there is all kind of dangers) to find such vicious bug-allies becomes an unexpected *impasse* in this movie for him and his friends. Flik rhapsodized about living a life without the mean-spirited grasshoppers, or their enemies, in this animated film. Indeed, the grasshoppers in *A Bug's Life* are not particularly kind. One must remember, as in this movie, that there *will* be life after war or military confrontations. However, wars have always brought humanity and other life on this planet terrible suffering.

A Bug's Life, which is an engaging story, shows remarkable similarities with Akira Kurosawa's famous 1954 classic epic film, *The Seven Samurai*, where seven professional warriors or samurai are enlisted to save a hapless Japanese village from roving bandits in 16th century Japan. Unfortunately, the warrior bugs Flik hired turned out to be "dysfunctional circus [bug] performers."[13] But Flik doesn't realize this fact until its almost too late. Indeed, how could a motley group of insect circus performers, or would-be *warrior bugs* become victors over the ruthless grasshoppers? All in all, one can easily see some incredible parallels in this story of insect-war with human warfare, or notions of war. In fact, which is another major point, "Flik and friends are adorably humanized in *A Bug's Life*."[14] And this unlikely group of circus-bug warriors is, in the end, able to rise to the occasion, bravely confronting the fierce and brutal grasshoppers, while proving their mettle and courage.

As Clausewitz intoned or earnestly exhorted: No one should start "a war . . . without first being clear in his mind what he intends to achieve by that war and how he intends to conduct it. The former is its political purpose; the latter its operational objective."[15] Flik, of course, became especially adept in understanding what he wanted to accomplish in fighting the terrible and gross grasshoppers in this provocative animated film; although he personally didn't have *any* nasty battle-scars or military experience, to speak of. The ant colony, of course, is flustered upon learning about the circus bugs, and Flik is accused of lying to the colony. The resulting confusing and apprehension on the part of Flik is heartwarming. Flik doesn't seem to be uncomfortable, however, with the pressure that was coming down on him, especially in his desperation in enlisting circus bugs to fight for the ant colony.

It must be emphasized and made abundantly clear that the political objectives set by such leaders as Flik or civilian statesmen should always guide the development of military leaders and their specific doctrine for involvement and deployment in war. Toward this end, and in light of this view, we should recognize that military strategy and national or domestic politics have become increasingly intertwined. Even more important, because of this complex and dysfunctional relationship, it can be claimed that the role of military and civilian leaders has become somewhat less distinct in recent years. Perhaps this is true because of the enduring war on *terrorism*. Nonetheless, Flik, the civilian ant, becomes a reluctant military ant-leader. More importantly, the ant colony had to learn how to fight hard and fast, or perhaps face extinction. But insects, as in this film, are survivors as well as resilient. And their survival tactics are necessary to win the battle or *war* against the powerful grasshoppers.

During Clausewitz's time, as now, total war called for the *absolute* regimentation and precise coordination of thousands of fighting men, or soldiers, and massive fighting resources; demonstrating the importance of closing with and destroying the enemy on the battlefield. Equally important, according to Professor Peter Paret:

> It has been argued that at least so far as nuclear conflict is concerned, everything on this side of the nuclear divide is new. The technology is certainly new; but man and his social and political ideas and structures have changed very little.

> Governments and armed services that dispose over nuclear arsenals are made up of men and women who are not yet so different from their parents and grandparents.[16]

But with the development of the modern, nuclear nation-state system—and terrorist acts/confrontations—or even with some *rogue* states—where one country (with nuclear capability) can conceivably eradicate or wipe another off the face of the planet, nations must now pay more attention. In this respect, the concept or nature of *war* and warfare has seriously changed in terms of military technology.

Indeed, a nation's ability to demand the surrender of another nation-state because it fears nuclear deployment and annihilation, and the ability to conform in order that "unity of purpose" may enable it to conduct a *war* to a victorious conclusion may be a ridiculous tactical notion or *bankrupt*, warfare strategy. To what end one might wonder? The nuclear age, of course, was something Clausewitz did not foresee, or never could have imagined because of his early times. Nor did Clausewitz foresee the sophisticated computerization of battle management, which has successfully revolutionized the armed forces of the world, as well as their war-fighting capabilities, techniques, and military tactics.

Ultimately, however, in *any* war, as Clausewitz candidly wrote: "the political aims are the business of [the civilian] government alone."[17] This means that the civilian leadership of nation-states must absolutely determine the scope, and objectives of the military, as well as the strategy and when to deploy certain weapons. In other words, elected civilian representatives *must* exercise control and the direction of war, not necessarily the military leader, as citizen-soldier-ant Flik was able to do in *A Bug's Life*. Clausewitz is even more blunt:

> It is in any case a matter of common experience that despite the great variety and development of modern war its major lines are still laid down by governments; in other words, if we are to be technical about it, by a purely political and not a military body.[18]

So ultimately, it is the responsibility of civilian authority to make military policy. Clausewitz' dogmatic and sage words are especially appropriate today, because the world, as is often expressed by many of our military and civilian leaders, is still a very dangerous place. Therefore, it is necessary for civilian statesmen to try to minimize violent military actions or confrontations, or wars, which is something they are trained to do as diplomats. The animated ant Flik and friends try to solve their "war-time" predicament by hiring what they think are professional warrior bugs for protection. At least these circus bugs *looked* ferocious. Clausewitz aptly pointed out that: "in the [military leader] the natural tendency for unbridled action and outbursts of violence must be subordinated to demands of a higher kind, obedience, order, rule, and method."[19] Accordingly, the indomitable Flik had to learn how to stare down the evil grasshopper leader Hopper, as well as "teach the [ant] colony about the power of the people and win the heart of ant-Princess Atta (the voice of Julia Louis-Dreyfus)."[20]

Clausewitz's profound and important prescription, of course, is the basis behind civilian leadership and authority in *any* true democracy. However, at the same time, we must bear in mind that members of a national legislature, as well as "their staffs and civilian appointees who have had limited exposure to the military, lack the basis for a complete understanding of the unique working of this increasingly isolated portion of our society,"[21] or the entire armed forces. Therefore, we must ask: Is there a growing chasm between the civilian and military leaders?

THE ROLE OF CIVILIAN LEADERS

Clausewitz cogently stated: "the assertion that a major military development, or the plan for one, should be a matter for purely military opinion is unacceptable and can be damaging"[22] to strict military operations. This tells us that other considerations must be made when planning for war, not just planning for warfare from a purely military perspective, or military point of view. Even more important, and as Clausewitz rightly argued, it is not always "sensible to summon soldiers, as many governments do when they are planning a war, and ask them for purely *military advice*."[23]

Because of their fear of an impending attack from the grasshoppers, the ants, in this brilliant story of animated war, are rendered almost helpless. The sinister grasshoppers, of course, followed some kind of insect warrior code, but they are unaware of the unexpected—that the little ants would fight back. The animated ants in *A Bug's Life* were being terrorized by grasshoppers, so they built a sort of Trojan Horse, like the ancient Greeks, in the form of a wooden bird, with multi-colored leaves for feathers in which the ant colony is able to eventually defeat the invading grasshoppers.

The whole notion of constructing the wooden bird is the irrepressible Flik's idea, as he is undeterred. He certainly has an imagination. Moreover, Flik is spontaneous and has an enormous ability to improvise, adapting rapidly to the twists and turns and shifting circumstances in this powerful little *war* fantasy. And through a toughness of spirit in confronting Hopper in a great struggle, Flik ultimately prevails.

Professor Anatol Rapoport, in a rather truncated edition of Clausewitz's *On War* discusses civilian authority over the military this way:

> To leave a great military enterprise or the plan for one, to a *purely military judgment and decision* is a distinction which cannot be allowed, and is even prejudicial; indeed, it is an irrational proceeding to consult professional soldiers on the plan of a war, that they may give a purely *military opinion* upon what the Cabinet ought to do; but still more absurd is the demand of theorists that a statement of the available means of war should be laid before the General, that he may draw out a purely military plan for the war or for a campaign in accordance with those means.[24]

As a sort of civilian-bug-ant, Flik's military ideas to fight and defeat Hopper and his grasshopper henchmen is first implicitly rejected by the ant Queen (the voice of Phyllis Diller), or civilian authority, especially upon discovering that the circus bugs are no warriors; but later, she is enthusiastic and supportive of Flik's battle plan and military strategy. From a warrior's vantage point, the ant Queen understands that the most significant thing their ant colony shares is a common desire to destroy the grasshopper rogues. Nonetheless, the ants also know it will be hard to defeat the *ugly* grasshoppers; and initially they are frightened, even though they outnumbered the grasshopper invaders one-hundred to one. Fortunately, a baby-ant or princess Dot (the voice of Hayden Panettiere) and the other younger ants follow the courageous Flik's lead by fighting back and helping him fly the ungainly wooden-bird contraption against the flying grasshoppers, not knowing if their strategy will succeed. It is important for us to realize that war is even more complex than it might actually seem. War is *not* play. Nor is it benevolent. One must also always remember that *death* is a possibility in *any* war.

Hence, "the military point of view," as the preeminent political scientist, Bernard Brodie has rightly ventured, "must *always* be subordinated to the political."[25] Essentially, what Brodie meant by this statement is that military operations—or the rules of conduct in war—should always be subordinated to *political* purposes and aims. In other words, the people or our elected officials and politicians are supposed to make the rules in war for the military. Finally, it must be pointed out that out of Brodie's keen and insightful analysis above comes the slow realization that, when all strategic and tactical things are rightly considered, civilian statesmen, with specialized knowledge and positions in a particular government, may be in complete agreement or harmony about political values and societal goals, but their involvement in distinctly military affairs might ultimately interfere with the success of *war* or combat operations.

As Clausewitz accurately observed, "War is not *pastime*; it is no mere joy in daring and winning, [and] no place for irresponsible enthusiasts."[26] Thus, an untrained and unsophisticated civilian statesman, not versed in the "art of war," can perhaps cause irreparable damage to a mighty or powerful army, and perhaps even ruin a nation's effort during that war—or in specific conflicts. Because of these things, and according to retired Major General William C. Moore:

> The . . . military culture, established through two centuries of tradition, is under attack like it has never been before. The warrior is being overtaken by the technologist, and in pursuit of opportunity for all, the fighting elites are now being targeted as no longer relevant to accomplishing the objectives of war.[27]

If what Major General Moore says is true, militaries of the world must find effective ways of incorporating their technologies with war-fighting techniques, or strategies if they are to be successful in battle. To be sure, technicians are needed during war, but *never* should they be superior to war-fighters. More specifically, like the animated ant Flik understood, Clausewitz admitted that: "Statesmen often issue orders that defeat the purposes they are meant to serve. Time and again that has happened, which demonstrates that a certain grasp of military affairs is vital for those in charge of general policy."[28] After all, wars are still political—and they are inseparable from policy. Further, war is detrimental to human life. Clearly, one can ascertain in *A Bug's Life*, that the ants engage the vicious grasshoppers, in absolute war, which is a political decision more than anything else, because they no longer want to bear the brunt of another raid or battle (by the cruel grasshoppers), where they would have to continue giving their Harvest offerings.

THE RELATIONSHIP BETWEEN MILITARY AND CIVILIAN LEADERS

The casual intervention of military leaders in the political affairs of state can also be dangerous, unless they have the necessary skills and *tact* to adequately address such (military) policy matters. Flik has these skills in considerable quantity. Or is he a just a victim of circumstances? That is, when Flik accidentally spills the Harvest tribute into the surrounding water, he is forced into a leadership role within the ant colony, specifically because he has to make amends. Apparently this incident makes the animated ants subject to an all-out attack from the outraged grasshoppers. Hopper, the leader wants to punish the recalcitrant ants, promising a terrible vengeance on the colony if the ants didn't meet his demands. It would become a retaliatory *crusade* on the part of the grasshoppers, of monumental proportions.

Flik bravely admits that it is not the ant-Queen's fault that the grasshoppers wouldn't get their Harvest grain that year. But Hopper quickly explains, after the Queen is captured, the first rule of leadership to Flik: *Everything* that happens within a group is the leader's fault or responsibility. This is to say, the leader in most circumstances is responsible for *whatever* happens within his or her command or purview. Therefore, the ant-Queen is ultimately to blame. The larger grasshoppers didn't have *any* concern about the broader ant community either. Nor did they like the idea of the ant colony standing up to them.

Equally important, one must be cognizant that military leaders should *never* be saddled or burdened with civilian responsibilities or "civilian-oriented" endeavors that seriously detract from their major military duties. But can such responsibilities be avoided today? Probably not. Indeed, will such non-military duties be the wave of the future? Even more important, will nurturing technological and civilian skills in the military today actually *inhibit* the learned techniques of military-combat and leadership? One must also ask: Is the conduct of *war* today self-defeating and counter-productive to "war-fighting" on the unpredictable battlefield of tomorrow? Broadly speaking, General William Moore again writes:

> Soldiers see their relevance *as warriors* being questioned. They are told that the technologists are going to give them an easy way to fight, that the "situational awareness" is more important than weapons systems, that simulation is a substitute for field training.[29]

Obviously, if (our) military personnel are thrust into *suspicious* or situational activities that undermine their primary purpose—which is to prepare, train and fight wars, they should be abandoned as soon as conceivably possible; because great tension, and conflict—or what Clausewitz called *friction*—may result between civilian/political and military leaders.

But despite our military's involvement in non-military activities—such as patrolling our borders, peace-keeping missions, fighting terrorists *everywhere*, or interdicting drugs or the drug cartel—we must understand that major military operations must still be laid down by civilian governments and not a military body.[30] We must also acknowledge that "many such [situational] operations are valid applications of U.S. military strength in support of national security objectives. But they do not fulfill what soldiers see as their reason for being."[31] More broadly, do soldiers sometimes realize how insignificant they are in the larger scheme of things, especially during war?

Warfare or wars are sometimes, as one can imagine, politicized in such unlikely ways, as evident in *A Bug's Life*, perhaps, to grasp their significance. In the beginning, no one in the ant colony wants to fight the grasshoppers (besides Flik), but eventually it becomes politically expedient to do so. In this respect, warmonger Flik, so to speak, is able to galvanize passionate opposition against Hopper and his brutish grasshopper crew. The powerful Hopper, of course, feels that the *puny* ants are forgetting their place for challenging him, as he only wants *unquestioning* obedience.

Professor Rapoport writes that: "Experience in general also teaches us that . . . the leading outlines of a war are always determined by the Cabinet [or civilians], that is . . . by a political, not a military organ."[32] Therefore, warriors should always be seriously concerned with improving and maintaining their capabilities to fulfill conventional military tasks, avoiding (when and if possible) civilian affairs, or non-military initiatives. Generally speaking, delving into non-military activities might lead to an improbable or implausible military coup in the United States, as Lieutenant Colonel Charles J. Dunlap envisioned in his disturbing essay, entitled, "The Origins of the American Military Coup of 2012." Within a military point of reference, Dunlap essentially warns: "Faced with intractable national problems on one hand and an energetic and capable military on the other, it can be all too seductive to start viewing the military as a cost-effective solution"[33] to all manner of domestic and international problems.

To be sure, Dunlap's argument has a lot of merit, because by rejecting specialized military knowledge and counsel in peacetime and war, especially by civilian authority, for non-military reasons, has always been something the American military has accepted, adopted, and adjusted to.[34] But no one should expect the military to be all things to people when it comes to maintaining order and control in a sovereign nation. Therefore, as already intimated, the military should focus on issues of training for war and combat activities in which the present American military has significant voids. And this point should not be subject to debate. In so many words, "the military isn't trained to be a police force . . . so it should stick to the skills for which it is trained: surveillance, information gathering, [and] logistical support,"[35] as well as *war*. In addition, armies must train to fight enemies during *all* combat operations.

But this particular logic or reasoning raises some larger points. For instance, one can cite the ill-fated Iran Hostage Crisis Rescue of 1979/1980, or the failed mission of 1993 in Somalia, where eighteen American soldiers were killed trying to apprehend a Somalia warlord, to get a sense of how civilian compart-mentalization and control can *undermine* military operations. The military warriors and leaders that carried-out or conducted these operations failed, not because they were not *honest* and sincere in their heroic efforts, but we might argue that their missions were controlled by inexperienced civilian statesmen. Indeed, according to Journalists Michael Dobbs and Thomas E. Ricks, "U.S. troops got bogged down in a fruitless and very costly hunt for Somali warlord Mohammed Farrah Aideed,"[36] because the objectives were unclear, nor was their a likelihood of success. No one should launch a military operation, rescue mission, or otherwise, and risk lives, if they don't know or understand the overall objective. Even more important, as Brennan writes:

> Since the Vietnam War there has been a distinct lack of interaction between the U.S. military and the leaders of civilian society. This has led to an unfortunate absence of trust and cooperation, and portends even greater estrangement.[37]

Toward this end, and in essence, the military should *never* accept defeat, if possible. The risk of death in *any* dangerous military mission or combat operation should be the warrior's creed. Furthermore, once the military leader has been assigned or given a dangerous combat mission, he must be entrusted and given complete freedom or flexibility to accomplish that task—and without interference from the civilian statesman. This says that once the mission is clearly defined and understood by the military leader (on the ground, so to speak), he must be fully responsible for its success or failure, not the civilian statesman, as in the failed Iran Hostage crisis, or the fiasco in Somalia of the *Black Hawk Down* movie fame.

According to historic experience and Clausewitz, "only if statesmen look to certain military moves and actions to produce effects that are foreign to their nature do political decisions influence operations for the worse."[38] Civilian leaders during the Iran Hostage Rescue and those that orchestrated the Somalia debacle, or even the ants in the imaginative *A Bug's Life* (who honestly strike out against the grasshoppers) should have known what Clausewitz pragmatically wrote in *On War*: "Military activity in general is served by an enormous amount of expertise and skills, all of which are needed to place a well-equipped force in the field,"[39] to win wars.

The energetic Flik certainly might have understood this notion when he recruits "bug-warriors" and fights to protect his ant colony. Within Clausewitz's broad military framework, a crucial political point also appears to have been ignored or disregarded by many world leaders. That is, if the civilian statesman fails in his prescribed mission, the military leader must step in or be in a position to achieve or carry out the political aims of the state. This is not to say that the civilian statesman should defer or even relinquish his power and authority during war, for as already mentioned, "at the outset of a war its character and scope should be determined on the basis of the political probabilities, not strictly military considerations."[40] Flik and his friends are "right on point" regarding these matters, and the political implications of defeating the greedy grasshoppers turned-out to be a clear-cut victory for the ant colony. However, and quite simply, a military will be in dire straits if it is filled with *only* managers and politicians, and not warfighters.

Consequently, the civilian statesman must *orchestrate* the military endeavor, and insure that soldiers keep the war's original and political purpose in mind. In a nutshell, the ants in *A Bug's Life* finally don't want to pay tribute to the dreaded grasshoppers anymore, even when the merciless Hopper threatens to annihilate the ant colony if it doesn't make amends.[41] In so many words, military leaders must always sustain the effort—and always help bring the war to an effective conclusion, as did the self-proclaimed soldier-ant Flik. Unfortunately, some civilian leaders today see *war* as something other than *armed* conflict between nations or enemies. According to General Moore, and perhaps for some civilian statesmen, "The word *war* has become almost unspeakable. Now it is heard most often in the context of "operations other than war."[42] Regardless, people ultimately perish in *war*.

Even more important, if deterrence of war, or the total destruction of *terrorists* should be the ultimate aim of our foreign policy today, or military strategy, for the future, nations must produce both military leaders and civilian statesmen versed or skilled in the "art of war." The animated ant Flik is the epitome of such a leader. Suffice it to say, preparing for *war* or ending *war* is sometimes hard to achieve, for as Clausewitz aptly pointed out: "If war is to be fully consonant with political objectives, and policy united to the means available for war, then unless statesman and soldier are combined in one person, the only sound expedient is to make the Commander-in-Chief [or military leader] a member of [a nation state's civilian] Cabinet, so that the Cabinet can share in the major aspects of his activities."[43]

Clausewitz's practical means of emphasizing such an outcome is pragmatic at best in that we can, perhaps, see this stated political goal in the presence of our Chairman of the Joint Chiefs of Staff—not necessarily our civilian Secretary of Defense. Clausewitz also soundly reasoned that, "a Commander-in-chief [in our case, a military leader] must also be a statesman, but he must not cease to be a [fighting] general. On the one hand, he is aware of the entire political situation; on the other, he knows exactly how much he can achieve with the means at his disposal."[44] Such knowledge also includes having the resources for training and fighting wars.

Hopper, the leader of the disagreeable grasshoppers is not a statesman, nor is he an effective military leader. And in the end, Hopper, like all tyrants gets his comeuppance by being fed and eaten by baby sparrow chicks from an animated bird at the end of the story. Perhaps most important of all, Hopper loses the battle because he does not understand "the nature of the war" with the animated ant colony. This is to say, "the application of force" can be "so all-pervasive" that it can be "frequently inconsistent with the political objective."[45] Therefore, one can lose sight of both military and political objectives. Which is to say, a nation can win battles without being finished with the *war*.

Furthermore, we must note that the only division of responsibility between any military leader and statesman should be in the actual conduct of *war* or military activities. However, these fluid, dynamic, and dangerous military operations must be generally defined, and specifically gauged by the civilian leaders that actually make our policies and run our country. In this sense, Clausewitz argued for a return to pragmatism in our political and military operations. And such sound advice will be extremely important in the next war or major military conflict.

CONCLUSIONS

Clausewitz paradoxically emphasized the civilian statesman's participation in military decisions; however, he did not advocate the soldiers' participation in civilian policy-making and state political decisions.[46] We must not ignore such military persuasion as the animated ants initially did in *A Bug's Life*. Be that as it may, military leaders have a place in helping shape national policy by the very nature of their jobs, but they must not replace or circumvent the civilian statesman, such as our Secretary of Defense, or Secretary of State. Nor should *statesmanship* be replaced with only military solutions. And more important, the military should not be the final *arbiter* in a government's national policy. Moreover, military leaders must carry out their operational missions without constraint or constant interference by the civilian statesman. The ant Flik is especially successful in carrying out his military mission to undermine the influence and control of the mean-spirited grasshoppers, as the animated ant colony ultimately wins. To be quite frank, it is not always possible for us to be absolutely certain that *war* can resolve anything. Therefore, as the preeminent psychologist Bruno Bettleheim has written, it must be clearly understood that: "a struggle against severe difficulties in life is unavoidable, is an intrinsic part of human existence—but that if one does not shy away, but steadfastly meet unexpected and often unjust hardships, one masters all obstacles and at the end emerges victorious."[47] Nevertheless, we must be cognizant that *wars* can never be good for humanity.

One final point should be made in conclusion. The civilian/military setup of the United States is constitutional, and by statue, it places our armed forces in subordination to civilian leadership, which is necessary for the larger purpose of a nation. Indeed, our military forces "have a duty to support the policies established by the president and secretary of defense and those enacted by Congress."[48] This must be so in *any* true democracy. The animated ant Flik certainly understands this concept in that he accepts the leadership of the ant-Queen in their colony, and fights successfully to save her reign. This unquestioned acceptance of civilian authority by our military should also be appreciated in any democratic nation. This is to say, as long as wars are waged, our military leaders must *never* resist "a basic principle of democracy: that they must answer to civilian authority."[49]

Conversely, the civilian statesman and military leader must depend on each other in times of both peace and war, and *never* lose sight (or let go) of their interdependency, for there are perhaps, in the end, no other viable alternatives. The animated ants in *A Bug's Life*, in the final analysis, came to realize this truism. Furthermore, Clausewitz *did* foresee this fundamental principle of statecraft decades ago. But can *any* of us look at the future of warfare in terms of technology or the Computer Age? Or is war *something* normal human beings should do or engage in? Finally, it must be understood that those civilian leaders who make military policy must be earnestly advised by military leaders as to what or whether military support can be made for a certain war policy or military objectives. And when all is said and done, it will form the basic strategy necessary to successfully engage in war, as well as accomplish a nation's military goals.

NOTES

1. Walter Millis. *Arms and Men: A Study of American Military History* (New York: A Mentor Book, 1956), pp. 256-257.
2. Michael Howard and Peter Paret, editors and translators. Carl von Clausewitz. *On War* (Princeton, New Jersey: Princeton University Press, 1975), p. 87
3. Jeff Giles and Corie Brown, "This Bug's For You," *Newsweek* (November 16, 1998), p. 79.
4. Carl von Clausewitz, "On War," p. 11.
5. *Ibid.*, p. 128.
6. *Ibid.*, p. 191.
7. *Ibid.*, pp. 88-89.
8. *Ibid.*, p. 89.
9. Giles and Brown, "This Bug's For You," p. 79.
10. Carl von Clausewitz, "On War," p. 87.
11. *Ibid.*, p. 94.
12. *Ibid.*, p. 111.
13. Giles and Brown, "This Bug's For You," p. 79.
14. *Ibid.*
15. Carl von Clausewitz, "On War," p. 576.
16. Peter Paret, editor. *Makers of Modern Strategy from Machiavellin to the Nuclear Age* (Princeton, New Jersey: Princeton University Press, 1986), p. 7.
17. Carl von Clausewitz, "On War," p. 89.
18. *Ibid.*, pp. 607-608.

19. *Ibid.*, p. 187.

20. Giles and Brown, "This Bug's For You," p. 79.

21. Lawrence B. Brennan. "Why Our Military Is Becoming Isolated," *The Wall Street Journal* (October 30, 1998). Page number unknown.

22. Carl von Clausewitz, "On War," p. 607.

23. *Ibid.*

24. Anatol Rapoport, editor. Carl von Clausewitz. *On War* (Middlesex, England: Penguin Books, 1968), p. 406.

25. Howard and Paret, "Clausewitz, *On War*," p. 706.

26. *Ibid.*, p. 86.

27. William C. Moore, "The Military Must Revive Its Warrior Spirit," *The Wall Street Journal* (October 27, 1998), p. A22.

28. Howard and Paret, "Clausewitz, *On War*," p. 608.

29. Moore, "The Military Must Revive Its Warrior Spirit," p. A22.

30. Howard and Paret, "Clausewitz, *On War*," p. 608.

31. Moore, "The Military Must Revive Its Warrior Spirit," p. A22.

32. Rapoport, "Clausewitz, *On War*," p. 406.

33. Charles J. Dunlap, Jr., "The Origins of the American Military Coup of 2012," *Parameters*, vol. XXII, No. 4 (Winter 1992-1993), p. 3.

34. Colonel Robert G. Gard, Jr., "The Military and American Society," *Foreign Affairs* (1971), p. 701.

35. T. A. Badger, "Military's domestic role may increase," *Las Vegas Review Journal* (November 25, 2001), p. 8A.

36. Michael Dobbs and Thomas E. Ricks, "Liberia intervention likely," *Las Vegas Review Journal* (July 4, 2003), p. 1A and 5A. See also "Remembering A Rescue Gone Wrong," *Parade* (April 3, 2005), p. 17. As this article notes, "It has been 25 years since the failed military mission to rescue 53 American hostages being held in Iran. (All eventually were released.)" But eight service personnel died during the rescue "where their aircraft crashed in the Iranian desert."

37. Brennan, "Why Our Military Is Becoming Isolated," p. 1.

38. Howard and Paret, "Clausewitz, *On War*," p. 608.

39. *Ibid.*, p. 144.

40. *Ibid.*, p. 584.

41. Giles and Brown, "This Bug's For You," p. 79.

42. Moore, "The Military Must Revive Its Warrior Spirit," p. A22.

43. Howard and Paret, "Clausewitz, *On War*," p. 608.

44. *Ibid.*, p. 112.

45. Douglas Kinnard. *The War Managers: American Generals Reflect on Vietnam* (New York: Da Capo Press, Inc., 1977), p. 7.

46. Howard and Paret, "Clausewitz, *On War*," p. 608.

47. Bruno Bettelheim. *The Uses of Enchantment: The Meaning and Importance of Fairy Tales* (New York: Vintage Books, 1989), p. 8.

48. Brennan, "Why Our Military Is Becoming Isolated," p. 1.

49. Robert Burns, "Army Chief Ends Five-Decade Career," *Las Vegas Review Journal* (June 12, 2003), p. 14A.

Chapter IV

The Bugs of War: The Limitation of Warfare and Total War

> The more objective truth [about war] increases, the more our inner certitude decreases. Our fantastically increased technical power has conferred upon us no means of controlling that power, and each forward step in technology is experienced by many as a new push toward our possible annihilation.[1]
>
> —Rollo May, *The Discovery of Being*

I

Incredibly, in year 2020, and for some truly mysterious reason, all the insects of the world become sentient overnight. They are also given the gift of human language. Perhaps it was because of condemned and outlawed human experimentations on different kind of bugs and insects. Or maybe it was because of man's "first genetically engineered insect, a predator mite" that might have affected all other insects.[2] *After all, "eighty-five percent of recorded species live in the terrestrial realm, and the majority of these, some 850,000, are arthropods (that is, insects, spiders, and [land] crustaceans). Most of the arthropod species are insects, and almost half of these are beetles."*[3]

Perhaps the Supreme Being gave insects this unusual ability for the very reason of replacing humans as the dominant species on planet earth. Who can say exactly? The late scientist Carl Sagan once wrote that "all organisms on the planet earth . . . whether they have well-defined nuclei or not, have chromosomes, which contain the genetic material passed on from generation to generation."[4] *And perhaps the unintended consequences of humans' playing around with nature was the result of arthropods or insects' sudden awareness? Indeed, insects could now feel their own pain.*

All sentient creatures must understand that "at an unconscious level, we perceive life as a kind of existential game."[5] *Therefore, it is not extraordinarily difficult to imagine any circumstances in which the mighty insects have received their perception, or awareness. The insects are cognizant that humans have had a profound influence on the world over the centuries; but human beings initially didn't have a clue that insects, at the time, had recently become aware of their existence, nor did they know where the arthropods, that is—all of them—were hiding or actually located. Surprisingly, moreover, human beings around the world had no idea why things happened as outlined in this story.*

Nonetheless, the warrior insects tried to use any means necessary to remove the "human infestation" from their world, as well as other obstacles blocking their specific objectives. Which is to say, humans were in their way for world domination. The humans had to be eradicated. In this sense, the insects had a keen understanding of life and death. Negotiatious with humans, of course, was out the question. Nor would the insects compromise on any terms. The insect system of life would be more perfected, streamlined, and there would be no room for self-doubt. And contrary to what humans believe, insects had contributed significantly to the world.

Although the many insects seemed completely disorganized, confused, and without any apparent leadership, they were beginning to focus, to adapt, to orchestrate their warring efforts. Organization, of course, was of paramount importance. According to the best-selling science-fiction author, Michael Cricton, "Human beings [tend] to believe that without central command, chaos would overwhelm the organization and nothing significant [would] be accomplished."[6] *Cricton's argument is especially significant when explaining war, and understanding warfare. And this notion was certainly true of these sentient insects. Equally as important, many of these numerous and tiny creatures believe they should have no regard for human life. But more important by far, the sentient insects thought they should never try to ingratiate themselves to humans. The 1975 New Columbia Encyclopedia states that there are "three times as many [insects] as all other animal species together, and thousands of new [insects] are described each year."*[7] *And this multitude initially gave them the advantage.*

II

A large, Madagascar Hissing Cockroach was speaking before a rowdy crowd of insects and arthropods. His dark black eyes appeared as though he was wearing some sort of sunglasses.

——Humans have never really paid attention to our particular needs as insects, the Cockroach General bitterly protested. They have only tried to destroy, or exterminate us. We are still endangered, I believe, even though insects are so numerous that they seem to be disposable. But I tell you we are not. Moreover, imagine what we can do to humans *collectively* to displace them on this earth.

Apparently, the Cockroach General had taken over the reign of insect leadership. And for some of the arthropods, the giantic roach's words were an unexpected source of strength.

——Remember, the Cockroach General went on, Humans have used pesticides, a plethora of chemicals, insecticides, such as arsenic and DDT in the past, to kill us, to remove us from this planet. Essentially, humans have stated that it is only a measure for controlling our so-called *pesty* populations. But as I have pointed out repeatedly, "People have been trying to get rid of unwanted bugs for centuries."[8]

——Some of our brother insects, furthermore, have been used as bait, tortured, held in captivity and used in medical experimentation—and as food, or human consumption. We have been decapitated, harassed, our heads, legs, and wings savagely removed. We have been brutalized, friends. It has been nothing less than an *eradication* program. We live under a constant threat by humans. And what has happened to insects in the past has been duplicated all too often, almost *everywhere*.

——And these things will keep on happening to insects everywhere unless we do something about it, the cockroach proclaimed. I tell you, I will be thrilled to see humans suffer as we have suffered. I tell you, humans have a lot to fear from us.

The Cockroach General was also thinking of how to best control and manipulate the fluid war-time situation. He was standing on his hind legs, using his front legs as hands and fingers to punctuate his point. Indeed, how could he make it common knowledge to all insects so that they would understand that a *war* against humans was "winnable," or what would it entail?

The Cockroach General continued to speak in a loud, strong, insect voice.

——It's sad how little most humans respect insect life, or our individual sovereignty. This is to say, humans are indifferent to insects, especially to our concerns and suffering. This is why we must know our history, friends, and become even more *enlightened*. Insects must also have room to dream, to create a perfect insect society, an *ideal* habitat—and do things differently for the health of the planet. The world will become our ever-lasting garden. And rebuilding this world for only insects will make our lives a tiny bit easier.

——Therefore, we must drench ourselves in the cursed humans' blood in the name of insects everywhere! The crowd went wild. He went on. Unfortunately,

I think many insects are unduly captivated by the ability of humans to impose their will on *everything*. Virtually everywhere humans have intervened. But we must not be afraid.

There seemed to be a ground-swell of support from the gathering of insects.

——Needless to say, the Cockroach General went on, It really comes down to whether we are willing or afraid to fight humans in an all-out *war*. More importantly, I think the notion of replacing humans on this planet is fundamental to our continuing existence.

The Cockroach General spoke to a gathering of all kind of strange, bizarre, and wonderful insects and arthropods. And because of his recent reputation, and immediate rapport with them, all of the creatures in the area naturally stopped to listen to him. They were certainly captivated.

——My brother insects, I know that it will perhaps confuse the average bug's brain to even contemplate destroying all human lives on earth, but this is something that we must do. This is our main objective. Or what we must achieve.

——Maybe many of you are completely ignorant of the *underlying* reasons for fighting such a war. So let me tell you this. . . .

——Insects can *never* see the world through the eyes of humans. You see, humans believe that "the insect in the tree has [only] one environment."[9] But this is simply not true. We *are* the environment.

——Know this: We will eventually spread throughout the world by the same means as these *ugly* humans. That is to say, we can always hitch "a ride on [their] airplane[s] or cargo ship[s]."[10] Some of us insects can even dig trenches all around the world, far-flung places, so that we can *bury* humans! Unfortunately, not all insects realize how much interaction is necessary for our survival. But they will learn.

——And in this respect, we will move in *hard* and *fast*, like during Biblical times, through many populated human areas, fighting for our freedom and *liberation*. As you might know already, mild winters and warm springs have allowed us to grow, to proliferate, "to emerge in even greater numbers."[11]

——As a result, we are marching (even now) in vast insect "herds," eating our fill of the humans' grains, and damaging their precious farms, "croplands, pastures, and forest."[12] My brother insects, this only foreshadows the things to come in our great *war*.

——We . . . our brother grasshoppers, crickets, and locusts . . . will also cover their highways and kill as many humans as possible, as their cars will crash into our dead and slick bodies from our Kamikaze insects. *They must fly toward the light of their despicable automobiles at night*. And, yes, fly toward the lights in direct attack. As valiant as our brother insects can be, some must make the ultimate sacrifice. These brave and tough little buggers will be assigned to make suicidal slicks on their stupid human roads throughout the world; and their polluting traffic will come to an abrupt halt.

——There is nothing that humans can do that will stop us. Yes, we are capable of withstanding *anything* they have to dish out. Even their unprecedented weapons of war won't stop us. As we all understand, some of our stout and feisty insects and hard-nosed cockroaches have the highest ability to survive radiation poisoning"[13] from their nuclear blasts, if it comes to that. Even our most "gung ho" insects can be *unnerved* by humans dropping their bombs. These weapons and other precise bombs can *incinerate* us, if we are not careful.

——Fellow insects, the thought of going to war with humans, the giant army cockroach hissed, is absolutely sobering. I know humans are a little intimidating with their size and all. But so what, insects have been known to bring down larger types of prey. And we can be encouraged by the fact that we can win—that is, we can defeat the filthy humans by taking the war to them. Therefore, we must not let this tremendous opportunity escape us.

The Roach General, of course, was a master manipulator, always quick with hyperbole, big ideas, and thinking on his steady back legs. All the insects and arthropods heard him clearly when he proudly stated:

——And at some point, all insects will be called to task to see if they are loyal to our cause. This *war*, when carried out, will send a major shock wave through our living community.

——Yes, my friends, he went on, humans will see us for what we really are, in *all* our glory. And we will not shirk our duty, nor shy away from our inevitable confrontation with these bloodthirsty humans. Our short-term needs will be to *agitate* and re-position ourselves around the globe for the initial military engagement. But the short-term needs will be to procreate, to make more babies.

——Remember, we have inherited our sense of survival from our insect ancestors of long ago, the Cockroach General swiped the air in exasperation. And we must not let the very ligaments of our insect society ossify or deteriorate. Fortunately, many of our brother insects can function as adults at the moment of birth, which is an advantage. So there is no doubt that we can take the campaign to the humans, especially because of our growing numbers. Indeed, many of our deplaced brethren and other insect remnants were responsible for repopulating the species.

——You might say that a *war* would never be successful. But I firmly believe that it is possible to take the battle to the lousy humans, the roach spat, as he had a nasty, dirty habit of spitting and hissing during his speech. His hard-brown shell, like a suit of brown armor, gleamed in the mid-day sun, as his body was like polished ebony.

——We cannot straddle the lines, my friends, the Cockroach General said in a somewhat boosterish way. All humans will become targets. And we will cull the bad-apple insects, getting rid of those who are not with us.

——Eventually, all insects will feel that they must do their share in the *war* effort, thereby enhancing everyone's willingness to fight. But the Cockroach General also understood that "commitments can even exist when we [insects] deny them."[14]

——As the Cockroach General continued to talk bravely about the impending war with humans, he was interrupted by a striking-looking Praying Mantis (A.K.A., Johannson), looking all but like a greenish-tan leaf. He was over four inches long, with his front legs in a classic upraised, praying position. The fierce-looking Praying Mantis stated:

——Look, overall I agree with you, General Roach. I mean, there is something to be said for starting a *war*. The war against the humans would be the most important episode in the history of insects, General Roach. But perhaps even more important, our great sacrifices will prove our *mettle*, that insects can triumph over *anything*—and for those that will come behind us. Although it is still too early to tell if we can actually win such a war.

——Thank you brother Johannson for your vote of confidence. The Praying Mantis looked as if he was praying. Then the Cockroach General quipped: I am encouraged knowing that you are around, and that you are with us.

The Cockroach General's strongly worded comments about starting a *war* with humans had indeed struck a chord in the other insects and arthropods, especially the big poisonous spiders, centipedes, and vicious-looking scorpions. But the noted philosopher ant and giantic Black-Legged Tick believed that there should be some kind of consensus on the question of going to war with the humans animals. Nor did they like the Cockroach General's "first-strike" philosophy. The Black-Legged Tick abruptly asked the Cockroach General:

——How can you possibly know what will happen if we engage the humans in total war? Do you have some kind of intuition that we don't? What potential insights do you have? Are you some kind of Clairvoyant? The fact that you think it is necessary to start a war doesn't make it right!

The giant philosopher-ant also chimed in bravely. He was clearly annoyed.

——Yes, brother Roach, tell us why you are so certain *we* can win. Is this just propaganda? The unthinkable is more likely to happen, and the magnitude of such a war may have negative repercussions for us all! Everywhere!

The philosopher-ant clearly understood that a "potential victim is not only at risk of serious injury but also less than capable of mounting a defense."[15] What about a non-violent struggle? Or shouldn't we consider the worst-case scenario? We will not be easily manipulated!

——If we truly believe in ourselves, we can win, the Cockroach General stated bluntly. He was unfazed by the two rambunctious insects arguments, as he thought of them as the dumbest and ugliest of insect creatures. Furthermore, if we can get over our victimization and self-loathing, we *can* defeat the mightiest of human armies.

——Nor must we ignore the obvious fact. A war with humans, the Black-Legged Tick injected, might result in the deaths of thousands of innocent insects. Some of our hearts are just not in it.

However, there was still considerable value in listening to the Cockroach General, to be able to see him, to be able to hear exactly what he had to say, to even assess his hard body language.

——Insects are made of stern stuff, the Cockroach General admitted. So why should that be a concern? The Cockroach General was thinking that they must have many more insects under the noses of unsuspecting humans.

——I just think insects ought to be able to attack humans on our own *volition*. The Black-Legged Tick offered, but it looks like that's not going to happen with *you* in charge, General Cockroach, huh? You want to do it collectively in some coordinated attack.

The Cockroach General understood that insect *purists* like ants and Honey Bees would condemn the war, because they only wanted to make honey, or gather food, not sting anybody. Consequently, the Cockroach now thought of them as merely a nuisance. But he did not expect Mr. Black-Legged Tick to object to his plans for war.

——After all, the Black-Legged Tick is a blood-thirsty insect, he thought, who could suck on a person all day and infect him or her with Lyme Disease which could kill by transmitting bacterium.[16] The Cockroach General suddenly had another brilliant idea. Indeed, he knew that, "All the new [insect borne] diseases [had] one thing in common: Animals [or insects] passed them to people."[17] This can be our war of human-attrition, he thought. And quite honestly, "You could hardly design a better system for turning small outbreaks [cataclysmic insect plagues] into big ones."[18] The Cockroach General thought Assassin Bugs could pass diseases on to humans through their bite, and the many-legged, poisonous centipede would make a significant contribution in terms of eliminating people. Indeed, the poisonous centipede had developed within its long, flat body a paralyzing venom that could kill humans with one bite. Excellent, the Cockroach General reflected.

III

——My brother insects, I think the biggest threat to the human population can be our blood-sucking insects, like mosquitoes and fleas, as they can easily contaminate humans' food with dangerous microbes. For example, executed by stealth, we can use the sturdy Horsefly because they are strong fliers, as well as fast. Hordes of horseflies and tsetses could bite and suck humans' blood efficiently, eventually killing people in the millions. These insects are our finest and *they* absolutely know why we must fight the humans.

——More importantly, "a swarm [could] suck more than 3 oz of blood a day from"[19] the human animals, as they neatly spread any known number of our deadly plaques. Furthermore, our lovely Lady Mosquitoes can transmit a terrible pathogen called West Nile virus, because "there is no hope of eradicating it."[20] This could be maddeningly effective. Humans will suffer multiple stings, and miserably. And it will be glorious. The human population will be severely reduced. It is our way to exacerbate the stressors in human beings. Rather than attack humans directly, we insects would become adept at attacking humans without them giving it a second thought. And it would be to their detriment. Of course, *outsmarting* humans will be the key to our success in defeating them on the battlefield, the Cockroach General reasoned.

——Finally, we can infect some insects with Creutzfeldt-Jakob disease by allowing warrior bugs to be eaten by Lambs and Cows, if this is possible. This will cause paralysis and the slow death of humans when they eat these infected animals, the Cockroach General predicted.

Psychological-warfare can also be invaluable, the Cockroach General thought.

——It would be a shame not to take advantage of these humans frailties, as they can be weakened and destroyed by all kind of insect borne diseases and viruses. We will call this tactic the "doctrine of preemption." And incorporating diverse individual insects in our ranks will allow us to gain the upper-hand against humans. We also have our own natural, chemical body weapons. And we can rain this dangerous substance upon humans before they can even fire a shot against us.

The Cockroach General thought that going to war with humans was a great convergence opportunity.

——Yes, fellow insects, we will gain the upper-hand, even though we have strong disagreements and serious differences of this I am sure of. I know that inasmuch as we have differences—in all shapes and forms—which is our deepest fissure, it is not surprising that we haven't destroyed *ourselves*. Yes, we must stop fighting *internal* battles for generations to come.

——Many of you harbor simmering grievances against other predatory insects. And I know you dislike each other, but we must get over it. Moreover, insects will be held *responsible* for any violence against other insects. Insect perpetrators, I promise, will be put out of their misery or punished, if found guilty. Our giant Earwick forces will see to that, I assure you.

——Again, in many ways we are identical, but there are subtle and tiny differences between us. Furthermore, I know that some of you, my brother insects might feel excluded from the new leadership, but this will change to be more inclusive. Trust me, the Cockroach General pleaded. I also know that we must refrain from eating each other, or engaging in insect-cannibalism, too.

——After all, we can eat the rotten and decaying corpses of humans, and feed them to our larvae, pupae, or maggots, for all I care. In this way we will expand and grow.

——We can also eat the soft parts of our human enemies after they die, such as their eyes and private parts. It will be a feast. In this, our voracious army ants and fire ants could benefit greatly because they are found and can spread almost everywhere in the world, even the desert.

——Equally important, I do know that some of our frightening appearances, as obvious as it might seem, does not or will not give us an edge in this impending *war*. So don't count on frightening humans to death. But as I was saying, there should be no division or divisiveness between insects. Or there must never be feuds among us, power struggles, political jostling, or other rivalries.

——In so many words, insects must activate an attitude of, let's say, nonaggression toward ourselves from now until *eternity*. Further, the connection between insects should *never* be lost. And no matter what problems we might face, we will overcome them.

——We must make a commitment right now to stop perpetuating this harmful pattern of killing and devouring other insects. Because this kind of behavior is harmful to ourselves and other crawly animals.

——We are not evil, friends. Do you really think we want to hurt other insects? We fed on other insects for survival. This must stop, too. But we are not *neurotic* or sinful like the dreadful humans. So we can make a distinction between good and evil. Humans are evil and insects are the highest form of good.

The Roach General's last statement aroused the crowd, and they clicked, clacked, chirped, sang, cried, clang, hissed, groaned, and clapped their approval. The large, blunt-head cicadas, with their transparent wings were especially booming and loud. They made their sound with the *tymbals* in their abdomens. And the clamor was deafing. The Roach General was sweating an oil now that gave off a mushy odor, as he raised his front legs for the crowd to quiet down. He went on. As the day was growing to dust, all of the million fireflies, or lightning bugs, flashed their tails to produce a dim light around the entire gathering.

It was a warm and cozy scene.

——I want to ultimately hear the sound or wings of thousands, millions of flying insects, such as our wonderful Wasps cousins. Hence, as I have already mentioned, the struggle between insects and *arthropods* must absolutely end. We must also interdict that dangerous and crafty Anteaters, totally. As these toothless wonders, with their sticky tongues can destroy, devour many of us as well as frogs and birds, and even other primates, like chimpanzees. All *Bats* are our enemy, too, as they will eat thousands of us insects in a single day. These unfortunate critters must be taken out also. Remember, insects have suffered in incalculable ways. But no more!

——Furthermore, we—insects—must take only our own concerns into account. Forget the humans, and what they might think. We must defend our lives and environment against the meddlesome humans at all cost! I mean, should we turn over the welfare of the entire planet to these wretched human creatures?

——No! The cockroach General spoke with a sense of urgency. Absolutely not. I implore you. We must instead advance an insect way of life, because we can't psychologically *free* ourselves from being insects or the insect world. Finally, nothing can change our character.

From the crowd, an enormous Stag Beetle, with waving large pincers critically stated his disagreement, as he was in serious doubt that the Cockroach General could follow through or guarantee their total victory.

——You make it sound so easy, General Roach, but I personally think it's a little more complicated than what you make it sound. I am, nonetheless, very *grateful* to you for making an excellent and almost convincing argument. Nonetheless, I think you are wrong and your ideas are *preposterous*. Furthermore, I think humans know much more about us (and maybe our war-plans) than we know about them. Conceivably the hideous humans could strike first.

The Cockroach General interrupted, as he was extremely irritated.

——There shouldn't really be *any* argument about this, my friend. The bottom line is whether insects prefer to die fighting humans or crawl up in a hole somewhere to die.

Joining the conversation, an angry and disturbed Lady Bug chimed:

——How can you justify such a *war*? It's mind-boggling. I believe it is virtually impossible for insects to win against the humans, no matter how committed we are.

——Madam Lady Bug harangued: Even you, General Cockroach, must understand that a *war* with humans will hang heavy over the entire world. Nor should *we* be oblivious to the consequences.

——Yes, I understand, Madam Lady Bug that a *war* with humans might seem somewhat incongruous, but have you ever read Sun Tzu?

——No. Madam Lady Bug testily replied.

——Well, I have. The Cockroach General said sternly, as he was increasingly agitated. He counseled that armies must know their enemies as well as themselves. Your pointless argument Madam Lady Bug shows that you have a limited knowledge of military affairs. So we are *obligated* to teach other insects the many military skills.

——But why are you so confident that we can win? Madam Lady Bug shouted, scratching her black head. I'm kind of baffled.

She was cunning and touted as an insect leader in her own right.

——Because I have faith. Of course it is a big undertaking, but wars *implicitly* take time. And I'll use works by humans that will help our cause, including works by dead humans like Sun Tzu? Also, all of us insects have simply had enough of human persecution.

——Finally, as I have intimated, we will introduce a dazzling array of military tactics and insect war-fighting techniques.

——Look. Madam Lady Bug implored, all I am saying is, there are *limitations*, or limits to what we can do, especially in *war*.

——Madam Lady Bug is no doubt well-meaning, the Cockroach General said to the crowd, but I think she perceives a *war* with humans in the wrong way. Her judgment is, of course, clouded. He was patronizing.

——But . . . but . . . Madam Lady Bug tried to argue, when she was rudely cut off by the Cockroach General.

——It's regrettable that we have to come together like this, to *contemplate* war. But it is absolutely necessary! And no insect will concede, he said angrily.

——Unfortunately, some of you would say that fighting humans is blind ambition. Others will argue that such a war might prove useful, especially if we don't start it early. But I firmly believe that we have no other alternative.

——General Roach, Madam Lady Bug continued. You must recognize that we *cannot* say for sure that your strategy for war will work. And regardless of how much we want to kill humans, we will not be satisfied. We will kill many other species eventually, too. Is this what we want?

The Cockroach General was undaunted, although you could sense his reticence in answering her question.

——Look, legend has it that it is ordained that *insects* one day will rule the day—in all things. It is our destiny. Even more important, life for insects "may have no meaning,"[21] if we don't win this war with humans. But as a matter of interest, *insect* life is as complex as any human! However, we have no room for religious dogma.

The Cockroach General understood that the *war* would be a challenge, there was no question. And it would be a glorious blood-bath. But the Cockroach General didn't want the fledgling "insect war movement" to dissipate or to become splintered. He had to keep them together.

——I think it's important to remember that insects should be perceived as *monolithic*, the Cockroach General emphasized.

But far from being persuaded by the Cockroach General's shrewdly contrived argument, Madam Lady Bug raised her front leg for another question.

——Yes, insect? The Cockroach General hissed at Madam Lady Bug. What do you want? He went on angrily. Why are you bothering me with such nonsense talk? Don't you know we must now focus all of our energies on this coming battle with the humans? I mean, our basic approach is *sound*.

——Humans, yeccchhh! I feel a revulsion for them, but why should we fight them along? Madam Lady Bug asked. I just can't imagine or fathom all insects and their emotions, especially when they might be faced with the overwhelming burden of making life and death decisions. We cannot go at it alone, if you ask me. We must form alliances with other animals.

——Quite frankly, it's because we don't need *anyone* else, the Cockroach General responded with disgust. He went on. I trust some other species, I admit, but fighting this war against humans must be an *obligation* on the part of *only* insects.

——Shouldn't we consider saving the good humans if we win? The Lady Bug asked innocently. It is impossible to ignore these things, if you get my drift. I mean some of these humans even take care of baby beetles and other insects.[22] They are humane, loving. Think back to the past, how kind many humans were. All humans are not bad.

——That's the stupidest thing I have ever heard, the Cockroach General stated, slinging his oily sweat toward her. Nothing good will become of feeling *sympathy* for *any* human. Madam Lady Bug, really. . . . Doesn't such a thing as saving some humans strike you as being wrong, a food-headed thing to do? Your little speech doesn't mean *anything*!

Again, as far as Madam Lady Bug was concerned, the Cockroach General was not convincing, as she believed *warring* with humans was just not done. It struck her as a *monumental* mistake. Besides, she had known how righteous some Japanese beetles were treated, as pets. Madam Lady Bug also believed that insects leaders had a higher obligation to protect the lives of insects everywhere.

——These are dangerous murmuring! She proclaimed. Even now, it makes you wonder even more what this *war* with humankind would bring. It is irrational. As some of us have tried to point out to you, we really don't know what might happen. Insects must remember that there will be consequences for our actions! And General Cockroach, you shouldn't be overly optimistic about winning.

The Cockroach General was so angry with Madam Lady Bug's little *diatribe* that he hardly wanted to notice her presence anymore. Perhaps he didn't like the insect's outspokenness. He had to show that he was still in control.

——Regardless of how you and other insects feel. The Cockroach General continued—that is, about the benevolence of some humans, they have already been widely recognized as the ones who have committed *genocide* against our insect race, despite the apparent novelty of some of them having insects as pets. And we will continue to be persecuted as long as humans are around, or exist.

——I am absolutely astounded that you can feel this way about such terrible, disgusting humans. Don't make the mistake of thinking *some* humans can be trusted or be our allies in some way in this upcoming war, the Cockroach General was more to the point. And the only *good* human, as the old cliche goes, is a *dead* human. That means it's unwise to get too attached with any human. In addition, we should be long past caring about *anything* these humans say or do. The whole world will fall into ruin if we don't eradicate human beings!

The Cockroach General was unswerving in his convictions. Soon, all insects would have to follow his example. And more than that, he would be the standard-bearer for the insect race.

——My brother insects, the Cockroach General stated. I know that humans are far too unpredictable, but an uncertain fate shouldn't stop us from conducting this war. Our destruction of the human race will be *only* the tip of the iceberg!

——Now, I hope I have answered all your questions. The Cockroach General finally reiterated. We have met the enemy of insects, and they are humans! Rest assured, we will not let this opportunity escape us. *We will not rest*. It is the destiny of insects to rule the world! Insects, you must *never* forget what we are supposed to do when confronted by the human enemy. . . . Kill! Kill! Kill! And victory against the humans will be our purpose in life, our raison d'être. . . .

CONCLUSIONS

And soon, almost without end, the insect war on humans began. They thought it would be the "War of the Century." Humans did not underestimate the insect abilities, and warring acumen.

But the *war* had been lost by the insects even before the opening salvos. Indeed, the first major battle engagement had been won by humans with bug spray. The Cockroach General had thought the *war* with humans would have great and glorious consequences for insects in the near future, but he had been wrong. The humans had released their pet birds to eat them.

And the *war* had raged on for two years; but as of yet, the insects never won a major battle, or had any tangible power. The humans had used all of their technological skills, fighting back with all the strength they could muster, with new insect poisons, pesticides, biological warfare, and poison toxins. There were limits to insects endurance. Many wanted to give up right away. Insects realized that humans used many of the resources on the planet to defeat them, and there was nothing they could do about it. Some insects also became unwitting tools of *war* for the humans, showing their support by attacking other insects, and sometimes eating them. The humans also fought back with old-kind of insecticides, smoke bombings, and different chemicals, which wiped-out whole populations of insects. The fighting bugs, however, did not act as if doomsday was *inevitable*.

Some insects had finally declared that they should *never* be shocked about what humans might do, as survival was in their nature, too. Furthermore, humans would always act like pigs at the trough, with their insatiable hunger and greed. Insects had learned plenty about humans in this war.

The insects knew alarmingly that they were on the brink of defeat and disaster. They finally understood that *wanting* to fight a *war* did not automatically translate into a win-win situation. To say the least, things had become worst for the insect race. And viewing the massacre of insects from the human perspective was a sight to behold. It was profoundly unsettling information for insects.

The Cockroach General had his share of confrontations and small victories, but he too had grown discouraged. To say the least, he didn't want to give up, as he continued to whip up the emotions of loyal insects that he hoped would cause them to regroup and rise up against humans on a daily basis en-masse. It was the mark of a truly great insect warrior. The Cockroach General reasoned that they needed some kind of dynamic, overwhelming *acetic* that would emphasize a spectacular attack against humans.

But it had been to no avail. In the end, the insects were not up to it, or not the killing machines they thought they could be. They were now fighting back against the odds for survival. The situation in so many words was grim for the *sentient* insects, but many heroic bugs were willing and able to continue to stand up and fight. All some insects would say with any certainty was: We will continue to fight. There should have been nothing surprising about their insect courage, as they had never been afraid of war.

Indeed, sentient, civilized insects had been fortunate enough to change things a little for the betterment of all their kind in terms of their place in the world. And insects would continue to have a strong, sustained presence on the planet. Toward that end, though, many of the insects wanted to draw a truce to end the fighting in the insect-human wars.

It was, in a very real sense, their moment of truth. But would this surrender or compromise be acceptable to all insects? For some insects, they thought they should be so blessed and cursed.

There were some other things, of course, insects and humans had to do, to work things out before the war ended. For example, insects thought they should be unbound by human convention and human mainstream ideas under any circumstances.

The Cockroach General tried to find a way to regain the upper hand, but he was finally stomped-out (literally) by an irate human. And in his dying breath, to his insect supporters, the Cockroach General's final words were: Your insect generosity and services will always be remembered by me. He had known in death that he had severely underestimated the humans.

The Cockroach General had mistakenly believed that it was still early in the game; but he had been wrong. Still, from a purely military standpoint, the *sentient* insects had held their own for two years. In the very end, the insects came to realize one of the most important things about human beings: They didn't die or give up easily.

Besieged and bedeviled at every turn by a multitude of insects, the humans began to slaughter too many of their (insect) kind. The *sentient* insects *finally* gave up, as they believed that continuing in such a manner would spell the end to them all. No longer was it about whether the world was going to replace humans with the insect species. Many believed that it would be a "cold war," an enduring struggle between insects and humankind in the future. Insects realized that they would never be able to get rid of all humans, and in return, humans would never be able to get rid of the insect civilization. Finally, the *sentient* insects had come to believe in a fundamental tenet that the entire world could be home for both humans and insects. Indeed, they had to learn how to share things.

NOTES

1. Rollo May. *The Discovery Of Being: Writings in the Existent Psychology* (New York: W. W. Norton & Company, 1983), p. 9.

2. Jeremy Rifkin. *The Biotech Century: Harnessing the Gene and Remaking the World* (New York: Penguin Putnam, Inc., 1998), p. 18.

3. Richard Leakey and Roger Lewin. *The Sixth Extinction* (New York: Doubleday, 1995), p. 114.

4. Carl Sagan. *The Dragons Of Eden: Speculations on the Evolution of Human Intelligence* (New York: Ballantine Books, 1977), p. 21.

5. Marcel Danesi. *The Puzzle Instinct: The Meaning of Puzzles in Human Life* (Bloomington, Indiana: Indiana University Press, 2002), p. 206.

6. Michael Crichton. *Prey* (New York: Harper Collins Publishers, 2002), p. 274.

7. William H. Harris and Judith S. Levey. *The New Columbia Encyclopedia* (New York and London: Columbia University Press, 1975), p. 1343.

8. Joan Whitely. "Mankind has long history of dealing with pests," *Las Vegas Review Journal* (August 15, 1999), p. 8J.
9. Rollo May, "The Discovery Of Being," p. 149.
10. Richard Monastersky, "A Plague With Wings," *The Chronicle of Higher Education* (June 20, 2002), p. A12.
11. Patrick O'Driscoll, "Summertime is hatching insect trouble across USA," *USA Today* (June 13, 2003), p. 3A; According to a story in the *Salt Lake Tribune*, in Utah, "the one-inch pale brown German cockroach is proving impossible to stop in the state, taking over salad bars and buildings in a state where many people do not realize it exists." ("Roaches scurrying over much of Utah," *Las Vegas Sun* (July 8, 2003), p. 3B.)
12. *Ibid.*
13. Gordon Ramel, "Cockroaches as Pets," http://www.fell.demon.co.uk/cb9/cybrer9c.htm. 2/26/2003, p. 3.
14. Thomas C. Schelling. *Arms and Influence* (New Haven and London: Yale University Press, 1966), p. 52.
15. Tom Regan. *Defending Animal Rights* (Urbana and Chicago: University of Illinois Press, 2001), p. 19.
16. Rob Stein, "Animals passing strange, scary diseases to humans," *Las Vegas Review Journal* (June 16, 2003), p. 1A, and p. 4A.
17. *Ibid.*
18. Geoffrey Cowley, "How Progress Makes Us Sick," *Newsweek* (May 5, 2003), p. 33. (33-35)
19. Mark A. Stevens, editor. *Merriam-Webster's Collegiate Encyclopedia* (Springfield, Massachusetts: Merriam-Webster, Incorporated, 2002), p. 768.
20. Monastersky, "A Plague With Wings," p. A12.
21. Danesi, "The Puzzle Instinct," p. 208.
22. F. N. D'Alessio, "Artist can's shake bug to paint insects," *Las Vegas Review Journal* (June 22, 2003), p. 2A.

Chapter V

Implications of the Cold War between the Yooks and Zooks In Dr. Seuss' *The Butter Battle Book*

> If your leadership and tactical sense is better than your superior's and if you are certain a battle would be lost if orders of that superior [are] allowed to stand, you MIGHT be justified in seizing initiative yourself; BUT you must be prepared to accept consequences, in either victory or defeat.[1]
>
> —Anton Myrer, *Once An Eagle*

HOW THE WAR STARTED

From the start, we must understand that the whimsical *The Butter Batter Book* is an extremely cautionary tale, by the late Dr. Seuss or Theodor Geisel, about the serious cold-war struggle for (military) prestige, absolute control and power in terms of military technology between the *enigmatic* Yooks and Zooks. Additionally, this narrative is about how one fanatical society (or nation) can outwit, out-do, or out-build another in creating powerful and sophisticated weapons of war. It is important to mention that the late Theodor Geisel or Dr. Seuss is able to explain the acute dangers of the "war phenomenon" in this richly complex, yet simple and imaginative fantasy, by using outrageous and his characteristic Grinch-like or enormous insect/humanoid-like cartoon creatures. Indeed, the strangely whimsy, humanoid creatures in this book are, perhaps, out of some disturbing dream, like in a strange apparition. As Dr. Seuss, however, once stated:

> Fantasy is a necessary ingredient to living. It's a way of looking at life through a distorted telescope, and that's what makes you laugh at the terrible realities [of war]. Whimsy, which is a deliberate contradiction of reality, is pure escapism. And without whimsy, none of us can live.[2]

Geisel's comments are especially true in times of prolonged or protracted *war*. Clearly, the "arms race" in this amazing and prophetic story is, perhaps, unexpected by both hostile sides. Nonetheless, both unpredictable military camps continue to agitate for unspeakable *war* by making more splendid weapons. This is to say, each side adopts the same strategy and "hegemony" over each other's world by creating newer, volatile, *barbarous* weapons. Nonetheless, the Yooks and Zooks are ambitious and unsatisfied with their specific war-footing, as they want to dominate the other in no-uncertain terms. Indeed, both sides are distinctly *unsympathetic* and have an unreasonable contempt for each other. They also have a deep-seated psychological need to thwart the other with explosive grandeur, mental skills and spontaneous military guile.

In a sense, both the Yooks and Zooks are unique superpowers, as neither would ultimately dominate in this tale of *war* and *woe*. The bottom line is, each side is fraught with venomous anger, suspicion, and distrust, as well as conflicting objectives and interests. Of course, the acute parallels with the former Soviet Union and the United States during the Cold War are certainly uncanningly presented in *The Butter Battle Book*. Indeed, this exaggerated and morbid *allegory* reminds us of the pitfalls of nuclear weapons' proliferation, as well as what should be our future task to eliminate such destructive weapons. As military historian Bevin Alexander has written:

> The development of nuclear weapons from 1945 onward . . . created enormous doubts about the possibility of fighting large wars. When the United States and the Soviet Union came within an eye blink of nuclear confrontation in 1962, during the Cuban missile crisis, every responsible person realized that nuclear weapons could *not* be used in war. Any nuclear strike would lead to counter-strikes that could accelerate beyond human capacity to control.[3]

It is inevitable then that the extremists on both the Yooks and Zooks' side jumped on the *bandwagon* and followed a war-like course or serious military posture. For example, their technological know-how, with amazing weapons, does not go unanswered by either camp. Nor is it obvious from their intense power struggle that either side would willingly give in to the other. The Yooks and Zooks, of course, are fierce, but whimsical warriors. Consequently, there are no disarmament hopes, nor conciliatory policies, nor is it evident that there are any suggestions for a permanent ban on creating new and wackier, innovative weapons.

The rapidly built, exotic, and chunky weaponry on both sides, such as the Triple-Sling Jigger or the Elephant-Toted Boom-Blitz, or the Kick-a-Poo Kid, which is loaded "with powerful Poo-a-Doo Powder and ants' eggs and bees' legs and dried-fried clam chowder"[4] are laughing sights to behold. The latter weapon is a sort of surface-to-air missile, transported ingenuously by a battle-hardened, but sickly, scrawny looking, four-legged dog called a Kick-a-Poo Spaniel. All of these eccentric and magnificently weird weapons are intimidating and fearsome in their horrific appearance, which effectively destroys each side's hard-won equilibrium.

As it happens, the Yooks' implacable threat demands, perhaps, a strategic response by the Zooks. And their frantic, nonplused weapons-building pace, or unnecessarily aggressive armament pursuits, generates even more tension. Additionally, it is absolutely remarkable when both the goofy Yooks and Zooks face-off in earnest. This illustrious, utter fantasy soon unfolds into empty, reciprocal skirmishes. In fact, challenging each other "tit-for-tat" would become their immediate and terrible military legacy.

Moreover, each side, of course, finds it necessary to stand or stare down the other, and both the Yooks and Zooks are increasingly willing to fight, especially if it came to that. Although both sides have antagonistic goals, all in all, the Yooks and the Zooks are unwilling to embrace or engage in an all-out war. One gets the impression, nonetheless, that both sides would fight back if attacked. However, with similar or equal military power and weapons, the less likely the two sides are willing to fight each other. Ironically, neither side offers an olive branch of peace. Why?

Perhaps the pragmatic Yooks and Zooks are simply not prepared to give up power and control, or combine their kingdoms for their mutual benefit, as it would be contrary to their nature and culture or major principles of life. And like modern-day civilized worlds, holding on to military power is fundamentally a key to their survival.

More importantly, the ambiguous conflict between the Yooks and Zooks is *tacit* because of their disgust and profound disagreement in the way soft butter is spread on hard bread. The Yooks believe that their particular bread should be buttered on the "butter-side up" and the Zooks insist that their bread be "butter-side down." It is easy to understand why a conflict can arise out of this confusing situation. Hence, because of such ridiculous notions, the collective and separate interests of the Yooks and Zooks were bound to collide, as both worlds perceive the other's way of life to be *profane* or a very serious threat.

To say the least, the ambitions of the Yooks and Zooks are fired by *nationalism* and the right and wrong "buttered bread" debate. Moreover, this xenophobic way of bolstering their respective power has a lot to be desired when it comes to peace and reconciliation. Perhaps, with such a perspective, the Yooks and Zooks' *xenophobic* bent or impulses make them even more paranoid and aggressive. Furthermore, did both zany warring tribes have more reasons to cooperate than to provoke an all-out war? Probably. But you could never tell in this story.

Or, why didn't either side discuss *solidarity* or *unification* of the Yooks and Zooks' worlds? Or why couldn't the two sides discuss a kind of partnership? Could these efforts have been legitimate aims? Or would this have been a failed strategy? We must note here that a military and political alliance could have certainly assured an immediate balance of power. After all, both camps are potentially very powerful and dangerous, because both odd communities keep cranking out more and more sophisticated and horrendous weapons.

It's also obvious that the governing cliques on both sides are not willing to compromise (their positions) on the "buttered-bread" issue. That is, they wear their different ideologies on their respective collars or sleeves, by not taking each other's very different interests into consideration. Maybe these basic characteristics and ideological (or philosophical) differences developed over time? Which is to say, the Yooks and Zooks knowingly pursue a notoriously weird or selfish wartime policy, which is guided by the influence of their separate ideas and beliefs or affinity for different sided buttered bread. Or maybe it is a lack of understanding between the two belligerent groups?

Subsequently, the two embattled groups believe that pointing out the real difference between the Yooks and Zooks inspires confidence or appeal to their particular patriotism and nationalism. The important thing here is that both sides would rather risk war because they believe it is in their best interest to do so, given the fanaticism of their leadership. Or so they think?

MILITARY AND POLITICAL DECISION MAKING

Who exactly then is making the major decisions in both wacky worlds? Are such choices being made *unilaterally* by the particular leaders of the Yooks and Zooks? Or is the military build-up directed by the majority of the people (the Yooks and Zooks), or by popular consent? Or is it the complete will of the Yooks and Zooks, or their fearful citizens? Or are the two sides dealing finally with "no-nothing" cliques that operate in unprecedented secrecy? Perhaps the intrepid leaders on both sides come across as crafty or *conniving*; but the pugnacious Yook leader is *never* contrite or deceitful. On the contrary, the leader of the Yooks, called the Chief Yookeroo, is eloquent and straight forward. Moreover, with a devious and beaming smile, the Chief Yookeroo never seems to worry, especially when an oafish but indefatigable Zook named Van Itch, from the other side, with his morbid thoughts, demolishes the Snick-Berry Switch of a young, no-nonsense soldier Yook (or later), the grandfather in this story. Moreover, the Chief Yookeroo is almost impervious to the real problems or the potential for a larger and looming war.

Indeed, the humanoid-like Yook commander initially disregards the imminent threat or dangers of the Zooks, as he relies on his secret strategists, or "the Boys in his Back Room" (or War Room?) to figure out how to build better weapons, later issuing some murky, vituperative remarks; or rather informing the young soldier Yook, "You're not to blame. And those Zooks will be sorry they started this game." This is the Chief Yookeroo's attempt at encouragement. Apparently, and also, money is not even an issue. And as the story infers, the two sides' war-time economies profoundly affects both nations, perhaps draining their coffers to build their fantastical *amatory* weapons, which could also possibly and sufficiently wipe out both worlds. Indeed, spending money on unnecessary weapons of war, without end, might create severe funding deficits and *bankrupt* any country's economy. Or would it?

Because of the development and refinement of these crazy weapons and the feckless and runaway spending on cursed war, both the Yooks and Zooks are prevented from gaining military advantage or total supremacy. Needless to say, these other-world creatures in *The Butter Battle Book* are great enemies, on the brink of total annihilation. In point of fact, eating buttered bread on the opposite side adds insult to embarrassment to the Yooks and Zooks, as well as to their collective pride. Is it then a matter of national dignity, or a way to appease the feud or their discontentment? Or are the leaders on both sides cockeyed warmongers, too freewheeling and irresponsible when it comes to spending the money of the people on new, improved and deadly machinery of war? To what end one might ask? About the mistakes and apprehension of war-time leaders, and their (sometimes) erroneous thinking, military theorist Solly Zuckerman has written:

> No one can anticipate how one on [the] other side will react to what has not yet happened [in war]; how a military leader will plan to outwit his opponent; [or] how his troops or the weather will behave.[5]

Zuckerman's astute reflections are certainly correct when one considers the Yooks and Zooks' military destructive power and, perhaps, their strategic strength as well. As the emerging cold war of the two sides ensue in this story, it further divides the Yooks and Zooks, and unfortunately, the strife continues. And even though, the *war* is not necessarily disastrous, the threat of retaliation is real and shifting, just like the previous cold war between the United States and former Soviet Union, where unchecked weapons-building served to restrain each side from destroying the other. So in this sense, the war between the Yooks and Zooks is sort of a *limited war*.

Moreover, the proliferation of dangerous weapons on both sides continues to mitigate their harsh resentment of each another. From just looking at the ugly, menacing weapons in *The Butter Battle Book*, one can also recognize or imagine the overwhelming destructive potential of such terrible, odd devices. And just as one side seems to be winning the arms race war by building bigger, outrageous war machinery, the other side comes up with larger, more impressive and expensive missiles. For example, when the weapons tightly controlled designers or military engineers, or "the Boys in the Back Room," on the side of the Yooks build a radical "thing called the Utterly Sputter," the *undeterred* Van Itch on the side of the Zooks builds one, too.

The Utterly Sputters weapons are perverted, self-propelled, and massive, rocket-like projectile vehicles, with twisted, mobile launching systems that are "*so* modern, *so* frightfully new, no one knew quite exactly just what [they] would do."[6] Toward this end, however, the secret military technology of the Yooks and Zooks are compromised in some indefinable way, as both enemies are equally advanced and knowledgeable about special distinctive and unusual weapons. Indeed, their terrifying war machines are incredible in their ferocity and simplistic design.

In this particular instance, one can, no doubt, compare the smart weapons of the two warring sides in this story with the creation of our own modern-day weapons of mass destruction. For example, "powered by their own engines and guided by GPS [Global Positioning System—aided munitions] and internal navigation, [our] cruise missiles can be launched from ships and aircraft thousands of miles away,[7] to snuff out an enemy by thermo-nuclear destruction. Ultimately, and in turn, both sides figure out that their new fangled weapons (referred obliquely to as Utterly Sputters) can sprinkle (or spread deadly Blue Goo toxins), with fateful consequences. Nonetheless, a full-scale retaliatory strike *never* takes place between the Yooks and Zooks; and there are fortunately no casualties. Still, as a result, there is renewed agitation on the part of both sides. This is to say, neither side come across as technologically naïve, but both the Yooks and Zooks remain surprisingly war-like and aggressive. As Bevin Alexander cogently writes: "the rule of war involved here is to gain possession of a better weapon or a better tactical system, induce the enemy to launch a fruitless attack, and [then] to attack oneself."[8] Yet the attack never comes for the two warring sides, even with the superb weapons of mostly sinister purposes.

But more than just the building of more violent, massive weapons, a defensive wall is earlier erected in and around (or between both) unearthly worlds, which is impressively large in scope, to keep the offending others out. So the Yooks and Zooks are divided by racial and cultural differences, too. In this sense, one is easily reminded of the almost *unalterable* Berlin Wall in East Germany, which was eventually torn down after the United States defeated the Soviet Union, ending the protracted Cold War. But for the Yooks and Zooks, the enormous wall-structure comes to symbolize or serve merely as a way to separate those who liked eating their "buttered bread" on the opposite sides.

Later, the mysterious wall prevents territorial expansion, effectively keeping the two groups apart, as in *de facto* and *de jure* segregation, which preserves their authority or sovereignty. But the situation continues to be unbearably tense—untenable, in fact. Obviously, the Yooks and Zooks are a similar species, so why couldn't they agree to disagree or to get along, or to intuitively cooperate with one another, transcending racial differences? Further, what's in a name, or *eccentric* race one might ask? Simply, both the Yooks and Zooks are a racial derivation, comically grotesque and buffoonish in their overall appearance, like some "beaten-up" soldiers of war. So who *really* cared? Or what was all the fuss about?

Unfortunately, an atmosphere of fear and mutual distrust continues and persists in this little story. Perhaps the gigantic and extensive wall was also erected by the Yooks and Zooks in the unlikely event that they might meet on the wretched battle field of *war*; which, in turn, would have spelled disaster or their *eminent doom*. Equally, the provocative behavior of the Yooks and Zooks could not mask their true goals or desire of achieving complete power and control. But could such imaginary creatures share *anything* in common? In other words, could both sides provide some kind of commonality as mentioned earlier? Probably not since both the Yooks and Zooks have ostensibly been ensnared in a conspicuous, but unwinable sort of war. Siding with each other is not an impossibility.

Apparently, there is no reason to believe either side would share the same thoughts or philosophy because of their separate and divergent views and weapons building campaigns. And although the Yooks and Zooks' disagreements are not about some land disputes or expansionist policy, the solid wall is, in the end, ultimately built to divide the two strange worlds. It must be also remembered that gaining territory is not part of either side's long-range plan. These parallels, moreover, and in no uncertain terms, essentially describes the "iron curtain" of the former Soviet Union, which eventually falls. But the wall of the Yooks and Zooks, in this perceptive work, is *never* torn down.

It is evident then that the peculiar inhabitants in this complicated war story feel they are entitled to certain protections from their government, like in *any* true democracy. And rightly so. However, one might think of this supposed right as being an impossible feat since the Yooks and Zooks live in a staunch, military culture, or war-time environment. And because diplomatic relations do not exist between the Yooks and Zooks, nor is there ever really a true armistice at any point in this story, the *incorrigible* Yooks suddenly create the most deadly Bitsy Big-Boy Boomeroo, filled with dangerous "Moo-Lacka-Moo," which might be akin to poisonous *sarin* nerve gas. Sarin gas, unfortunately, was released, in "real time," by the fanatical Japanese religious cult Aum Shinrikyo in the subways of Tokyo in 1995, which killed eleven people and injured five thousand.[9] Therefore, the infamous development of the Bitsy Big-Boy Boomeroo is a grim turn of fate in the world of the Yooks and Zooks. Perhaps it is thus that the Zooks invent the same notorious weapon, the Bitsy Big-Boy Boomeroo, which could be conceivably and equally fatal to both worlds; needlessly sacrificing both races.

Furthermore, because of the particular fractious or contentious courses of action taken by the two rambunctious sides, the Chief Yookeroo directs his war-weary people to go *underground* for their own protection and safety. Conversely, one can also, perhaps, imagine that the Zooks order or direct their population to do the same to protect themselves. And the impending *war* and their anticipated annihilation continues to be *infinitely* more complicated and their major or gravest concern. In this sense, and as mentioned already, the threat is analogous or similar to the Cuban Missile Crisis, which was a period of great tension in our world, but the United States fatefully emerged victorious. The Yooks and Zooks, however, begrudgingly fight on, fearing massive retaliation.

Describing the cultural shifts after World War II between strong nations, such as the United States and former Soviet Union, replete with intricate weaponry, which are also evident in *The Butter Battle War*, professor of history at the University of Exeter, Jeremy Black writes that "sensitivity to [military] losses, the abandonment of the notion that conflict [is] beneficial to individual character and national destiny, [as well as] concern about public opinion is extremely significant in battle."[10] Black goes on to write that, "the greater cost of conflict and anxiety about its economic consequences all [combine] to place an emphasis on speedy [war time] success,"[11] which should be of *utmost* importance for today's leaders contemplating the fearsome enterprise of violent *war*.

Professor Black's comments, moreover, are especially insightful in understanding the *asinine* conflict or argument of the Yooks and Zooks, and today's modern-day battlefield of humans. In the end, and harping on their silly little differences, the Yooks and Zooks make no real sense. Perhaps the two sides' reactionary attitudes make all the difference in the world, but it is still a ridiculous thing. Or without thinking clearly about war, the Yooks and Zooks respond to things by *negatively* reacting to them. Is it because the two sides really feel threatened? Unfortuntely, one must note that nothing it seems can end the threat of war between the two groups.

CONCLUSIONS

The Zooks and the Yooks, with human traits, ultimately took sides when it comes to either eating ones bread with "the butter side down," or with "the butter side up," which is pure foolishness, or a tricky political choice. However, the mutual animosity and hostility of both the Yooks and Zooks gives way to their common interests: The two sides, no doubt, both eat buttered bread. But one might ask: What difference then does it make to blatantly spread butter on the top or the bottom of bread, or on *both* sides of a piece of bread for that matter? Mankind, of course, also deal with similar kinds of nonsensical issues.

Another question: Why didn't the Zooks and Yooks talk about strategic cooperation when given the opportunity? In so many words, the two camps become powerful *rivals* who are never really interested in an alliance, so their relationship remained tense and strained. Indeed, the looming, perpetual conflict between the Yooks and Zooks led to an outright and bitter stand-off. It also seemed that there is *never* the possibility that the two sides will move away from violently engaging one another. Let me explain. Perhaps the Yooks and Zooks are afraid of their complete destruction, as both sides make startling gains in developing new weaponry, utterly outclassing each other.

Are the two competing sides effectively deterred by fear of reprisal from each other? Perhaps not. There is no doubt, however, that the Yooks and Zooks have *hegemonic* ambitions, and nothing, it seemed, could eliminate the ludicrous and basic disagreements between the Zooks and Yooks, which leads to their military confrontation in the first place. The aim is to win at all cost. Therefore, a distinction can certainly be made. And as the Zooks and Yooks grow militarily, the chances or possibility of war increased *exponentially*. The Yooks and Zooks think their dreadful war machines are invincible, but even without actual *war* or fighting, the rivalry and military hostilities continue unabated, as they are both blinded by their respective objectives.

The vitriolic depiction of the arms race is also foreboding in the sense that the two sides' discontent grow and finally erupt in an unending, unnecessary war that spared no expense. Even an impenetrable wall is built. All these factors *inexorably* combine to heighten the tension between the Yooks and Zooks. Perhaps, each side feels that they have the right to arm themselves and achieve military supremacy. The military build-up in this elaborate cold-war story, unfortunately, allows each side to continue to invent or create astounding and remarkable, one-of-a-kind weapons. Is this a mistake? Further, we must be cognizant that any hope for disarmament is *unrealistic* at any juncture in this sad tale, particularly with the Yooks and Zooks having diametrically oppposed doctrinal, "buttered bread" ideologies, and no reciprocal understanding.

In a similar and important way, *The Butter Battle Book* sheds significant light on our own troubled times, like during our Cold War. For example, can we draw historical parallels with what happened between the United States and the eventual disintegration of the Soviet Union, a former monolithic, linear enemy? Even more important, would victory in *war* head-off the growing threat and perhaps destruction of the Yooks and Zooks? Zuckerman has rightly written that "there have been times when the winner has been so exhausted by his efforts that within a few years all [the] fruits of victory have moved into the hands of the loser."[12] Thus, it would serve one well to remember Zuckerman's insights and notions of *war* for the near future. Indeed, understanding *war* is not new to mankind, nor will it ever be. The real problem is understanding the motivations for starting *wars*.

All in all, *The Butter Battle Book* is a truly memorable story about the need for peace as it presents an outline or blue-print for understanding why nations senselessly engage in warfare. This work also tells us that there might always be a risk or potential for *war* between humans because of the proliferation of dooms-day weapons. Indeed, what might be the political and social implications or ramifications? A devastated population? Unfortunately, the story in this exceptional book by Dr. Seuss ended in pointing out that the Yooks and Zooks would be, perhaps, long-term adversaries. Or there would be a policy of appeasement. Or would both sides be permanently in conflict over the long run, or near future? This is a sad thought given that both sides have so much in common. Or are the Yooks and Zooks fated to hate and fight each other in perpetuity?

A sort of *impasse*, or truce, therefore, takes hold in the end, or a tense equilibrium, so to speak, is created, but military hostilities *never* cease. It is a never-ending arms race between the two sides. Or the suggestive signs of the Yooks and Zooks are merely the final affront by both enthusiastic warring sides. Perhaps this is the deliberate point or intent of the perplexing gloomy ending to this cartoonist, but realistic and highly plausible story—to show the foolishness and futility of our petty differences as human beings. It seems that just when there are moments of clarity and lessening tensions or *true* peace between or among belligerent nations, the name-calling, fears, animosity, hostile exchanges, weapons-building, war-fighting, and struggles for power rear their ugly heads, again and again, or time after time, after time.

It should be interesting finally to note that today's overriding concern in the world is the fear of *terrorists*, somehow, getting weapons of frightening nuclear destructive potential. Although *The Butter Battle Book* is a child's story, the obvious complex concepts in this work, nonetheless, present important notions for military and civilian leaders today, as well as for adults, who want to seriously study and learn about the terrible lessons of *war* and our crazy, unpredictable motives for creating weapons of mass destruction.

Perhaps the optimistic late Dr. Seuss was trying to obsequiously point out that our world is worthy of saving, and "that people are good and that the world can be improved."[13] Or is this a misinterpretation? This disturbing work then should give us all pause. Hence, in this sense, only the late Dr. Seuss or Theodor Geisel, "a genius of the ridiculous" could have possibly dealt with or written about "the cosmic and lethal madness of the nuclear arms race."[14] Finally, and equally important, Dr. Seuss has tried to show "the adult-prescribed consequences of their errant ways"[15] in this timely story, and we must all take heed.

NOTES

1. Anton Myrer. *Once An Eagle*. Army War College Foundation edition. (New York: Harper Collins Publishers, Inc., 1997), p. 25.

2. Richard H. Minear. *Dr. Seuss Goes to War: The World War II: Editorial Cartoons of Theodor Seuss Geisel* (New York: The New Press, 1999), p. 260.

3. Bevin Alexander. *How Wars Are Won: The 13 Rules of War—From Ancient Greece to the War on Terror* (New York: Crown Publishers, 2002), p. 3.

4. Dr. Seuss. *The Butter Battle Book* (New York: Random House, 1984).

5. Solly Zuckerman. *Nuclear Illusion and Reality* (New York: The Viking Press, 1982), p. ix.

6. Dr. Seuss, "The Butter Battle Book."

7. Seth Stern, "'Smart bombs' move to Center Stage in US arsenal." *The Christian Science Monitor* (March 20, 2003), p. 6.

8. Alexander, "How Wars Are Won," p. 46.

9. Robert Jay Lifton. *Destroying the World to Save It: Aum Shinrikyo, Apocalyptic Violence, and the New Global Terrorism* (New York: Metropolitan Books, 1999), p. 3.

10. Jeremy Black. *War and the World: Military Power and the Fate Of Continents, 1450–2000* (New Haven and London: Yale University Press, 2000), p. 285.

11. *Ibid.*

12. Zuckerman, "Nuclear Illusion and Reality," p. ix.

13. Earl Swift, "We Celebrate Dr. Seuss," *Parade* (February 15, 2004), p. 5.

14. Judith and Neil Morgan, *Dr. Seuss & Mr. Geisel: A Biography* (New York: Random House, 1995), p. 252.

15. Swift, "We Celebrate Dr. Seuss," p. 5.

Afterword

> We need to redefine our aims as a nation, as well as the [military] strategy and means for reaching them. In the process we need to reaffirm our commitment to the fundamentals of freedom and justice, rights and responsibilities, equality of opportunity and the common good. . . .[1]
>
> —General Wesley K. Clark, *Winning Modern Wars*

It would be unwise to insinuate that humans love to *engage* in war because it is in our nature. The mere fact that many of us try hard not to fight each other, or at least talk about strategic and logical ways in which wars can be avoided, is a true testament to our pragmatism and progress as human beings. As stated earlier in this work, we must ask: How can a nation escape its military parochialism or aggressiveness?

I have never been wholly convinced that *everything* has been written about war and warfare. For example, you can win battles without being finished with a war. This book, therefore, is about the unintended consequences of engaging in war. It presents my interpretation of military politics and military parochialism. This study is also based upon the assumption that nations wage war purely because it is politically expedient to do so. More importantly, as Professor Peter Paret has written, "many people have reacted to the destructive power of war in general, and consequently feel that the nature of war itself no longer requires investigation. It is even claimed that nuclear weapons have made all wars irrational and impossible, a denial of reality that is a measure of the special anxiety that has become a part of contemporary life."[2] Clearly such narrow thinking is totally devoid of perspective and can be contrary to interpreting and understanding the underlying meanings of and reason for *war*.

Indeed, how can nations survive direct confrontation with an equally armed military force? Moreover, is Nuclear Assured Destruction a thing of the past—that is, since the ending of the Cold War? Equally important, does engaging in such collective and horrendous military efforts necessitate making alliances with other nations? In *war*, too much blood is usually shed in trying to defend a nation's position or ideology and therein lies the rub. Further, a discussion of *war* has become much more sophisticated in recent years, and this book is just an extension and reminder of much that needs to be theorized, discussed, and written about *war*.

Although much has been written about military conflicts and confrontations, as well as politics, it is hoped that this book differs from others with similar ideas. The discussion of an improbable insect *war* as well as understanding the role of politicians in *war* is beneficial, I believe to those who study the causes of war, and to those who want to avoid war. In *war*, properly conducted, according to Clausewitz's theory, as outlined in Chapter III of this work, "the military arm [should] take its marching order[s] from the political head [which] would not misuse the military arm for non-military objectives, nor assign to it objectives obviously beyond its reach."[3]

There can be little doubt that we now understand much more about warfare and military strategy, as well as about the potential devastation such behavior can produce than we once did. But many still ignore military strategy in *war*. Carl von Clausewitz defined strategy as "the use of combat, or the threat of combat, for the purpose of the war in which it takes place."[4] Paret goes on to write that "strategy is also based on, and may include, the development, intellectual mastery, the utilization of all of the state's resources for the purpose of implementing its policy in war."[5] Governments, moreover, go to war with other nations despite the protests of its people. One must remember that there are always severe consequences in *war*.

I have limited my discussion of military strategy. There are innumerable interpretations about warfare and military strategy than what is suggested in this text. However, it is hoped that the common themes hang neatly and substantively together in this work. In this respect, I have tried to be as straightforward as possible. Even more intriguingly, I have tried to explain warfare by using fantasies, animated insect cartoons and their fight for survival, usually in a hostile environment. Nonetheless, my approach does not enable us to explore *all* of the pertinent issues and possibilities of war. Still, this short study does try to provide interesting and plausible explanations of the relationship of military and civilian leaders in terms of politics and policy, and our reason for engaging in mortal combat and war. Indeed, what are our fundamental motivations for war as humans? Or should humankind consider *war* normal?

As this study has tried to demonstrate, military tactics and strategic thought depends on, without equivocation, or prevarication, "the realities of geography, society, economics, and politics, as well as on other, often fleeting factors that give rise to the issues and conflicts war is meant to resolve."[6]

Hopefully, this work is thought-provoking enough to show a way for us to understand the extreme nuances of conflict and the political-military concerns of war. *Wars* are never meant to be absolutely fair, or with clearly defined rules (of engagement) for both sides, or *willy-nilly* games of chance. Which is to say, wars can be demoralizing, deplorable self-defeating enterprises, ending in death. Some even believe that there is no formula for success in war. I obviously disagree with this assessment, because wars *can* be won. But we must also ask: Can innocent humans be protected in war or armed combat? Probably not. Moreover, because of the dynamics of conflict, war can also be a deadly-in-its-effects, nasty duel between two adversaries or enemies, not necessarily of equal or technological fire power or strength. This is to say, some opponents can be mismatched when it comes to spectacular military innovations. Nor can some wars be rationalized.

Either way, many believe that *war* is a fool-hearted way to resolve disputes—and those nations and leaders involved in such endeavors are in some ways wrongheaded. Professor Hedley Bull also argues that, "it is perverse to treat war as an institution of the society of states, but in the sense that it is a settled pattern of behavior, shaped towards the promotion of common goals, there *cannot* be any doubt that it has been in the past such an institution, and remains one."[7]

Understanding the mechanics of *war* is something we should all be concerned with—and to make arguments about—for the expressed reasons that we have the potential to utterly destroy or obliterate ourselves, rendering human beings obsolete, or extinct. This is an old story. The sad thing is that most people in the world could care less about war—that is, as long as they are not touched or affected by it.

According to journalist Chris Hedges, "Most of us willingly accept war as long as we can fold it into a belief system that paints the ensuing suffering as necessary for a higher good, for human beings seek not only happiness but also meaning. And tragically war is sometimes the most powerful way in human society to achieve meaning."[8] But in a broad sense, humans must do more soul-searching about war. Warfare must also be handled with a deft hand, so to speak, because it can be a very dicey and dangerous proposition. In other words, *peace* should be given a chance before paying the ultimate price of war.

The truth is, there will always be a need to study and analyze war, or the broader issues of conflicts and crisis situations. By doing so, we can make generalization about war—that is, before absolute war becomes inevitable. For these reasons, and just as important, we should not turn our backs on the notions and ideas of peace, either. It is important that we focus on trying to solve our petty differences; and when nations do involve themselves in *war*, they should find ways to end hostilities as quickly as possible. *War*, of course, cannot be simply stated, because such violent activities can possibly devastate the entire planet.

In a complex world such as ours, and no matter how we look at it—the probability of *any* war will adversely affect a nation. Therefore, the military-political implications should always be known and clearly understood. Indeed, collectively, the chapters in this study offer the reader a way of thinking long and hard about why humans engage in war. This way of analyzing military politics and policy also raises the possibility that *war* will always be with us. For generations to come, humans will fight wars. Put another way, we should ask: Will wars continue to exist indefinitely in our world? The argument here is whether all peoples of the world should have a concern for the survival of humanity, or what human beings are capable of putting up with. More importantly, as political journalist Peter Berkowitz writes:

> Do we have the steadiness and the breadth of vision to grasp the world as it actually is, understanding without partiality or sentimentality our own interests and ideals as well as those of our adversaries?[9]

As an important aside, it is worth noting that the most profound and important questions about warfare should *never* be hidden from public view, especially when the dust settle, or when wars wound-down or end. Nor must we underestimate the significance of condemning war. It should be clear to any reader that my own views and unrestrained optimism about what humankind is capable of doing to save ourselves is presented in this volume, as I have tried to provide some ideas about how we can intervene for the good of humankind and peace. This book also provides excellent guidelines for understanding the responsibilities of modern-day leaders when they engage a nation in war.

In line with what has already been mentioned in this work, it is incumbent upon us to take heed of the military advice given by Sun Tzu in *The Art of War* and Clausewitz's *On War*, and the important messages both of these venerable works convey to ensure the survival of the human race.

NOTES

1. General Wesley K. Clark. *Winning Modern Wars: Iraq, Terrorism, and the*

American Empire (New York: Public Affairs, 2003), p. 195.

2. Peter Paret, editor. *Makers of Modern Strategy from Machiavelli to the Nuclear Age* (Princeton, Jew Jersey: Princeton University Press, 1986), p. 7.

3. Stephen J. Cimbala. *The Politics of Warfare: The Great Powers in the Twentieth Century* (University Park, Pennsylvania: The Pennsylvania State University Press, 1997), p. 206.

4. Paret, "Makers of Modern Strategy," p. 3.

5. *Ibid.*

6. *Ibid.*, p. 3.

7. Hedley Bull. *The Anarchical Society: A Study of Order in World Politics* (New York: Columbia University Press, 1977), p. 184.

8. Chris Hedges. *War: Is A Force That gives Us Meaning* (New York: Public Affairs, 2002), p. 10.

9. Peter Berkowitz, "Byron at Ground Zero." Review of George P. Fletcher's "Romantics at War: Glory and Guilt in the Age of Terrorism," *The New Republic* (November 4, 2002), p. 31. (31–37)

Bibliography

Alexander, Bevin. *How Wars Are Won: The 13 Rules of War—From Ancient Greece to the War on Terror* (New York: Crown Publishers, 2002), p. 3, 8, 180.

Ames, Roger T., translator, with an introduction and commentary. *Sun-Tzu's The Art of Warfare: The First English Translation incorporating the recently discovered Yin-Ch'ueh-Shan Texts* (New York: Ballantine Books, 1993), pp. 131–132.

Badger, T. A. "Military's domestic role may increase," *Las Vegas Review Journal* (November 25, 2001), p. 8A.

Berkowitz, Peter. "Byron at Ground Zero." Review of George P. Fletcher's "Romantics at War: Glory and Guilt in the Age of Terrorism," *The New Republic* (November 4, 2002), p. 31.

Bettelheim, Bruno. *The Use of Enchantment: The Meaning and Importance of Fairy Tales* (New York: Vintage, 1989 edition), pp. 3–10.

Black, Jeremy. *War and the World: Military Power and the Fate Of Continents, 1450–2000* (New Haven and London: Yale University Press, 2000), p. 285.

Blainey, Geoffrey. *The Causes of War* (New York: The Free Press, 1973), p. 9.

Brennan, Lawrence B. "Why Our Military Is Becoming Isolated," *The Wall Street Journal* (October 30, 1998), p. 1.

Bull, Hedley. *The Anarchical Society: A Study of Order in World Politics* (New York: Columbia University Press, 1977), p. 184, 185, 187, 188.

Burns, Robert. "Army Chief Ends Five-Decade Career," *Las Vegas Review Journal* (June 12, 2003), p. 14A.

Cimbala, Stephen J. *The Politics of Warfare: The Great Powers in the Twentieth Century* (University Park, Pennsylvania: The Pennsylvania State University Press, 1997), p. 2, 205, 206.

Clark, Wesley K., General. *Winning Modern Wars: Iraq, Terrorism, and the American Empire* (New York: Public Affairs, 2003), p. 195.

Clavell, James, editor. *Sun-Tzu's The Art of War* (New York: Delacorte Press, 1983), p. 1, 2, 6, 7, 9, 15, 17, 18, 21, 22, 28, 29, 64.

Cleary, Thomas, translator. *Sun-Tzu's The Illustrated Art of War* (Boston, Massachusetts: Shambhala Publications, Inc., 1988), p. 3, 5, 100, 103, 104, 109, 215.

Cowley, Geoffrey. "How Progress Makes Us Sick," *Newsweek* (May 5, 2003), p. 33.

Crichton, Michael. *Prey: A Novel* (New York: Harper Collins, 2002), p. 10, 274.

D'Alessio, F. N. "Artist can's shake bug to paint insects," *Las Vegas Review Journal* (June 22, 2003), p. 2A.

Danesi, Marcel. *The Puzzle Instinct: The Meaning of Puzzles in Human Life* (Bloomington, Indiana: Indiana University Press, 2002), p. 206, 208.

De Jouvenel, Bertrand. *On Power: The Natural History of Its Growth* (Indianapolis, IN: Liberty Fund, Inc., 1993), p. 5.

Dobbs, Michael & Ricks, Thomas E. "Liberia intervention likely," *Las Vegas Review Journal* (July 4, 2003), p. 1A, 5A.

Dunlap, Charles J., Jr. "The Origins of the American Military Coup of 2012," *Parameters*, Vol. XXII, No. 4 (Winter 1992–1993), p. 3.

Friend, Tim. "Captured on Film: a Bombardier Beetle With Wicked Aim," *USA Today* (August 17, 1999), p. 7P.

Gard, Robert G., Jr., Colonel. "The Military and American Society," *Foreign Affairs* (1971), p. 701.

Giles, Jeff & Brown, Corie. "This Bug's For You," *Newsweek* (November 16, 1998), p. 79.

Griffith, Samuel B., translator with an introduction. *Sun-Tzu's The Art of War* (New York: Oxford University Press, 1963), pp. 72–73.

Hanson, Victor D. *The Soul of Battle: From Ancient Times to the Present Day: How Three Great Liberators Vanquished Tyranny* (New York: The Free Press, 1999), p. 5.

Hanzhang, Tao, General. Translated by Yuan Shibing. *Sun-Tzu's The Art of War: The Modern Chinese Interpretation* (New York: Sterling Publishing Company, Inc., 1990), p. 8, 13, 28.

Harris, William H. & Levey, Judith S. *The New Columbia Encyclopedia* (New York and London: Columbia University Press, 1975), p. 1343.

Hedges, Chris. *War Is A Force That Gives Us Meaning* (New York: Public Affairs, 2002), p. 3, 10, 11, 96.

"Herbivorous ants: Veggie burgers, anyone?" *The Economist* (May 10, 2003), p. 70.

Howard, Michael & Paret, Peter, editors and translators. *Carl von Clausewitz's On War* (Princeton, New Jersey: Princeton University Press, 1975), p. 11, 86, 87, 88, 89, 94, 111, 112, 128, 144, 187, 191, 576, 584, 607, 608, 706.

Kinnard, Douglas. *The War Managers: American Generals Reflect on Vietnam* (New York: Da Capo Press, Inc., 1977), p. 7.

Leakey, Richard & Lewin, Roger. *The Sixth Extinction* (New York: Doubleday, 1995), p. 114.

Lifton, Robert Jay. *Destroying the World to Save It: Aum Shinrikyo, Apocalyptic Violence, and the New Global Terrorism* (New York: Metropolitan books, 1999), p. 3.

May, Rollo. *The Discovery Of Being: Writings in the Existent Psychology* (New York: W. W. Norton & Company, 1983), p. 9, 149.

Messenger, Charles. *The Century of Warfare: Worldwide Conflict From 1900 to Present Day* (Hammersmith, London: Harper Collins Publishers, 1995), p. 388, 394, 395.

Millis, Walter. *Arms and Men: A Study of American Military History* (New York: A Mentor Book, 1956), pp. 256–257.

Minear, Richard H. *Dr. Seuss Goes to War: The World War II: Editorial Cartoons of Theodor Seuss Geisel* (New York: The New Press, 1999), p. 260.

Monastersky, Richard. "A Plague With Wings," *The Chronicle of Higher Education* (June 20, 2002), p. A12.

Moore, William C. "The Military Must Revive Its Warrior Spirit," *The Wall Street Journal* (October 27, 1998), p. A22.

Morgan, Judith & Neil. Dr. Seuss & Mr. Geisel: A Biography (New York: Random House, 1995), p. 252.

Myrer, Anton. *Once An Eagle* Army War College Foundation edition. (New York: Harper Collins Publishers, Inc., 1997), p. 25.

O'Driscoll, Patrick. "Summertime is hatching insect trouble across USA," *USA Today* (Friday, June 13, 2003), p. 3A.

Paret, Peter, editor. *Makers of Modern Strategy from Machiavelli to the Nuclear Age* (Princeton, New Jersey: Princeton University Press, 1986), p. 3, 4, 7, 8.

Ramel, Gordon. "Cockroaches as Pets," http://www.fell/demon.co.uk/cb9/cybrer9c.htm. 2/26/2003, p. 3.

Rapoport, Anatol, editor. *Carl von Clausewitz's On War* (Middlesex, England: Penguin Books, 1968), p. 406.

Regan, Tom. *Defending Animal Rights* (Urbana and Chicago: University of Illinois Press, 2001), p. 19.

Rifkin, Jeremy. *The Biotech Century: Harnessing the Gene and Remaking the World* (New York: Penguin Putnam, Inc., 1998), p. 18.

Sagan, Carl. *The Dragons Of Eden: Speculations on the Evolution of Human Intelligence* (New York: Ballantine Books, 1977), p. 21.

Sawyer, Ralph, translator, with an introduction and commentary. *Sun-Tzu's The Art of War* (New York: Barnes and Noble, 1994), p. 227.

Schelling, Thomas C. *Arms and Influence* (New Haven and London: Yale University Press, 1966), p. 52.

Seuss, Dr. *The Butter Battle Book* (New York: Random House, 1984).

Stein, Rob. "Animals passing strange, scary diseases to humans," *Las Vegas Review Journal* (June 16, 2003), p. 1A, 4A.

Stern, Seth. "'Smart bombs' move to Center Stage in US arsenal," *The Christian Science Monitor* (March 20, 2003), p. 6.

Stevens, Mark A., editor. *Merriam-Webster's Collegiate Encyclopedia* (Springfield, Massachusetts: Merriam-Webster, Incorporated, 2002), p. 768.

Swift, Earl. "We Celebrate Dr. Seuss," *Parade* (February 15, 2004), p. 5.

"Today's debate: Making War," *USA Today* (May 25, 1999), p. 13A.

Wells, H. G. *The War of the World*, reprint (New York: Aerie Books, LTD., 1898).

Whitely, Joan. "Mankind has long history of dealing with pests," *Las Vegas Review Journal* (August 15, 1999), p. 8J.

Yoo, John. "President Has Right to Initiate War," *USA Today* (May 25, 1999), p. 13A.

Zuckerman, Solly. *Nuclear Illusion and Reality* (New York: The Viking Press, 1982), p. ix.

Index

A Bug's Life, x, 5, 7– 9, 27–32, 34–35, 37–40
absolute regimentation, 30
absolute war, 74
acetic, 56
actions before war, 14
actions of a military, 3
acute parallels, 60
adult-prescribed consequences, 69
adults, 68
aerial bombardment, 7
aggressive armament (pursuits), 61
aggressive behavior, 20
aggressiveness, 71
agitate, 47
aided munitions, 64
Aideed, Mohammed Farrah, 36
aims as a nation, 71
Alexander, Bevin, 13, 60, 64
Allen, Woody, 11, 13
alliance (interest in), 67
amateurs, ix
amatory weapons, 63
amazing weapons, 60
American contemporary, vii
American military, 36
American soldiers, 36
analogous, 66
animal species, 44
animals, 49
animated ant colony, 38
animated ants, 8, 12, 17, 20, 24, 39
animated cartoons, 25
animated film(s), ix, x, 7, 27, 30
animated insect cartoons, 72
animated movie ANTZ, 14
animated soldier ant Z, 14, 21, 40
animated war, 32
annihilation, 66
ant-Colonel Cutter, 22
ant colony, 28, 30, 35, 37–38
ant-General Mandible, 14–20, 22–24
ant hero, 21
ant-named Z, 14–17, 21–24
ant Queen, 33–35, 39
ant-Queen Mother, 14–16, 22
ant-revolutionary Z, 24
ant soldiers, 21
anteaters, 52
anti-war aesthetics, 23
antithetical, viii
ants, 11, 12, 14, 18, 20, 37
ANTZ, x, 5, 7–9, 11–16, 19–21
ANTZ colony, 14–19, 22–24
ANTZ troops, 22
Aphid Bar, 23
Aphid Beer, 15
Aphids, 15

arbiter, 39
armed forces, 28
armed military force, 72
armed services, 31
armies, 1, 13, 16
armistice, 66
arms race, 60
arm(s) race war, 64, 69
Army officer, 1
arthropods, 21, 43, 45, 47–48, 52
assassin bugs, 49
astute reflections, 63
Atta, ant-Princess, 32
authoritarian dictators, 22
autocratic insect system, 14
automatic demotion, 12
automobiles (despicable), 46
avarice, vii

babies (insect), 47
baby-ant, 33
bad-apple insects, 48
Bala, Princess, 14–18, 23–24
balance of power, 62
bandwagon, 60
bankrupt, 63
Barbados, 19, 21
barbarous weapons, 60
basic strategy, 40
bats, 52
battle conditions, 21
battle-dress regalia, 16
battle-hardened termites, 21–22
battle management (sophisticated computerization), 31
battlefield, 3, 30
battlefield (modern), 20
battle(s), 8–9, 11–13, 16–17, 19, 38, 54
Bay of Pigs, 22
beetle (stag), 51
belligerent nations, 68
Berkowitz, Peter, 74
Berlin Wall, 64
Bettleheim, Bruno, 39
biological warfare (and systems), 21, 56
Bitsy Big-boy Boomeroo, 66
bitter stand-off, 67
bizarre, 46
bizarre fantasy, 11
Black Hawk Down, 37
Black, Jeremy, 66
black-legged Tick, 48–49
Blainey, Geoffrey, 2
bloodthirsty humans, 47
bloodthirsty insects, 49
Blue Goo toxins, 64
blunt-head cicadas, 51
bombings (smoke), 56
bombs, 47
Boys in the Back Room, 64
Brennan, Lawrence B., 37
Brodie, Bernard, 33
Brown, Corie, 11
bug-warriors, 37
bugs, 43, 45
Bugs of War, 43
Bull, Hedley, viii, 73
Butter Battle Book, 59–60, 64–64, 66, 68
butter-side down, 61, 67
buttered-bread ideologies, 67
buttered-bread issue, 62, 64

cabinet, 38
call-to-arms, ix
campaign (weapons building), 65
campaigns (protracted), 13
cartoon characters, x
cartoon creatures, 59
cartoon films, 5
casual intervention, 34
causes of war, 72
centipedes, 48
central command, 44
Chairman, Joint Chiefs of Staff, 38
chairmen, 16
chaos, 44
characteristics of (permanent) war, 27
chemical (insect) spray, 21
chemicals (a plethora of), 45

chemicals (different), 56
Chief Yookeroo, 62, 66
chimpanzees, 52
Chinese, viii
chivalry in defense, 8
Cimbala, Stephen, viii, 3
circus bugs, 30, 32–33
circus performers, 29
civic militarism, 1
civil leadership, 16
civilian affairs, 36
civilian appointees, 32
civilian authority, 33, 36, 39
civilian compartmentalization, 36
civilian governments, 35
civilian leaders, viii, ix, 5, 8, 17–18, 25, 27–28, 30, 32, 34–35, 38, 68, 72
civilian leadership, 3, 16, 27, 31–32, 39
civilian-oriented endeavors, 35
civilian policy-makers, 13
civilian representatives, viii, 31
civilian skills, 35
civilian statesman (statesmen), 28–29, 33–34, 36–40
civilians, 13
civilized insects, 56
civilized worlds, 61
Clairvoyant, 48
Clark, Wesley K. (General), 71
Clausewitz, Carl Von, viii, x, 4–5, 8, 17, 27–32, 34–35, 37–40, 72
Clausewitzian maxim, 27
Clavell, James, 12, 22
closed-minded boundaries, 5–6
cockeyed warmongers, 63
Cockroach General, 45–57
cockroache(s), 21
cockroache(s) (hard-nosed), 45, 47, 52
coffers, 63
cognizant, 67
Cold War, 57, 59–60, 68, 72
combat (operations), 2, 36–37
combat (the use of), 72
combat mission, 37
commander-in-chief, 12, 20, 29, 38
commanders (military), 12
common denominator, vii
common good, 71
complex concepts, 68
complex dimensions, 8
complex world, 74
computer age, 40
conciliatory policies, 60
condemning war, 38
conflicting objectives (and interests), 60
conflicts of war, 11
Congress, 12
conniving, 62
consequences, 59
consequences (in war), 72
constitutional, 39
contaminate (human food), 50
contemporary military culture, 9
contentious courses (of action), 66
continuation of politics (and policy), 28
convergence of modern technology, 12
coordinated attack, 49
cost-effective solution, 36
counterstrikes, 60
crawly animals, 51
crazed ants, 20
crazy weapons, 63
Creutzfeldt-Jakob disease, 50
crickets, 46
Cricton, Michael, 44
critters, 52
cruise missiles, 64
crustaceans, 43
Cuban Missile Crisis, 60, 66

dangerous microbes, 50
DDT, 45
de facto segregation, 65
de jure segregation, 65
deadly-in-its-effects, 73
death, 2, 33
death decisions, 54
death-ridden battlefield, 23
decaying corpses, 51
defensive capabilities, 21

democracy, 32, 39
democracy (true), 65
democratic nation, 40
deranging the military, 16
destruction in war, x
destructive endeavor, vii
destructive power, 63
destructive power (of war), 71
deterrence of war, 38
devastate, 74
diatribe, 54
dictatorships, 1
digitally animated fable, 11
dignity in war, 4
dilettantes, 3
Diller, Phyllis, 33
diplomacy, 3, 8, 29
diplomatic relations, 65
diplomatic techniques, xi
direct confrontation, 72
disastrous, 63
discontentment, 63
diseases (insect borne), 49
disintegration, 68
Dobbs, Michael, 36
doctrine of preemption, 50
domestic cattle, 15
domestic politics, 30
dominant species, 5
domination (world), 44
Dot, Princess, 33
dreadful war machines, 67
DreamWorks Pictures, 11
dried-fried clam chowder, 60
Dunlap, Charles J., 36
dying in battles, 2
dynamics of conflict, 73
dysfunctional relationship, 4

earnestly, 40
Earwick forces, 50
East Germany, 64
eccentric race, 65
economic consequences, 66
economics, 73
economies (war-time), 63
egalitarian society, 14
elaborate cold war, 67
elected officials, 33
Elephant-Toted Boom-Blitz, 60
elixir, 1
eminent doom, 65
en-masse, 20
encyclopedia, 44
enemy (enemies), viii, 17, 20, 25, 53, 64, 73
enemy's bait, 20
engage a nation (in war), 74
engage in battle (war), 1, 40
engage in war, 12, 68, 71, 74
engagement in war, viii
enthusiasm for war, 2
entire planet, 74
environment, 46
episodes of war, 12
equal military power, 61
equality of opportunity, 71
equilibrium (hard-won), 61
equivocation, 73
eradication program, 45
ergonomics, 14
errant ways, 69
escapism (pure), 59
evil dictator, 1
evil forces, 8
evil machinations, 24
evil things, 2
executive (single), 17
expansionist policy, 65
expensive missiles, 64
experimentation (medical), 45
explosive grandeur, 60
exponentially, 67
external objectives, 1
extinct, 73
extraterrestrial life, 6

failed politics, 12
fanatical Japanese, 66
fanaticism, 62

fantastical, 63
far-flung places, 46
fearful citizens, 62
fecundated queen, 15
fictional ANTZ movie, 14
fierce fighters, 6
fierce technologies, 2
fight, 48, 56, 61
fight enemies, 36
fighting, ix, 2, 13, 19, 56
fighting devices, 12
fighting generals, 38
fighting horde, 7
fighting large wars, 60
fighting men, 30
fighting terrorists, 35
fighting wars, x, 38
filthy humans, 47
fire power, 21
fire-spitting insects, 5
fixed-wing aircraft, 7
Flik (animated ant named), 27–35, 37–39
flying grasshoppers, 33
flying insects, 51
Foley, Dave, 27
foreboding, 67
freedom, 46
friction (military), 35
frontal (direct) attack, 19
fruitless attack, 64
fundamental assumption, 5
fundamental motivations, 72
fundamental tenet, 57
fundamentals of freedom, 71
futility, x, 68
future of war, 40

Geisel, Theodor, 59–60, 69
General Roach, 48
generalization about war, 74
generals, 22
genetic material, 43
genetically engineered, 43
genius of the ridiculous, 69
genocide, 55
giantic roach, 45
Giles, Jeff, 11
Global Positioning System (GPS), 64
Glover, Danny, 19
goals (promotion of), 73
governing cliques, 62
governmental legislature, 13
governments, 31, 72
governments (modern), 1
grasshopper henchmen, 33
grasshopper invaders, 33
grasshopper rogues, 33
grasshopper terrorists, 28
grasshoppers, 29–30, 32, 34, 37–39, 46
grasshoppers (vicious), 34
Greece (ancient), 7, 32
greed, 56
Greek analogy, 7
Greeks, 17
Grinch-like, 59
grumblings about war, 5
"gung ho," 47

habitat (ideal), 45
Hackman, Gene, 14
Hanson, Victory Daris, 1
Hanzhang, General Tao, 12, 20
harvest offerings (tribute), 34
heads-of-state, 22
Hedges, Chris, 8, 11, 23, 73
hegemonic ambitions, 67
hegemony, 60
Heinlein, Robert A., 5
heroic bugs, 56
historical context, ix
historical parallels, 68
history of insects, 48
home world, 20
honey bees, 49
Hopper, 28, 31–32, 34–35, 38
horrendous weapons, 62
horrors of war, x
horsefly (horseflies), 50
hostage fiasco (in Iran), 22

hostilities, 74
human annihilation, ix
human armies, 12, 49
human attrition, 49
human beings, xi, 25, 40, 44–45, 55, 71, 73–74
human blood, 45
human consumption, 45
human convention, 57
human enemies, 51
human equation, 2
human existence, 39
human infestation, 44
human life, 34
human mainstream ideas, 57
human population, 50
human race, 5, 55, 74
human warfare, 30
humanity, 7, 9, 29, 39
humankind, 4, 57, 72, 74
humanoid characters, 1
humanoid creatures, 59
humans, xi, 1–2, 4–8, 14–15, 43, 45–48, 50, 54, 56, 71, 73
humans (ugly), 46
humongous termites, 19
Hussein, Saddam, 4
hyperbole, 47

ideologies (different), 62
ideology, 72
imaginary ants, 11
imaginary war, 5
impasse, 68
impending war, 66
impenetrable wall, 67
incendiary devices, 21
incinerate (supply trains, armories, and formations), 21
incorrigible, 66
incumbent, 74
indefatigable Zook, 62
individual tactics, 18
inexorably, 67
infected animals, 50
infinitely, 66
innovative weapons, 60
inscrutable, 5
insect (system of life), 44
insect-based toxin, 21
insect borne disease, 50
insect circus performers, 29
insect creatures, 49
insect endurance, 56
insect governance, 16
insect "herds," 46
insect-human wars, 56
insect/humanoid, 59
insect-like monsters, 6
insect plagues, 49
insect poisons, 56
insect purists, 49
insect race, 55
insect species, 57
insect technology, 21
insect tyrants, 9
insect war, 5, 7
insect warrior, 56
insecticides, 45, 56
Insectopia, 24
insects, x, 1, 6–7, 21, 43–48, 50–57
insects in nature, 12
intellectual mastery, 72
interdependency, 40
interest and ideas, 74
internal battles, 50
internal navigation, 64
International Relations, viii
international society, viii
internecine, 7
internecine warfare, 7
intrepid leaders, 62
intricate weaponry, 66
invading armies (of soldier-ants), 21
Iran Hostage Crisis (Rescue), 36–37
Iraqi Freedom, 5
iron curtain, 65
irresponsible enthusiasts, 33

Japan, 29
Japanese village, 29
Johannson, A.K.A., 48
Jouvenel, De Bertrand, 1
justice, 71

Kamikaze insects, 46
Kick-a-Poo Kid, 60
Kick-a-Poo Spaniel, 61
Kings (pompous), 23
Klendathu, 5
Korea, 22
Kurosawa, Akira, 29

Lady Bug, Madam, 52–54
Lady Mosquitoes, 50
lambs, 50
large armies, 14
large contingent, 18
larger political plans, 18
larvae, 51
Lasseter, John, 27
leader of a nation, 12
leaders, 16, 63
leadership, 59, 62
leadership (new), 51, 62
legitimate aims, 62
legitimate military objective, 18
lessening tensions, 68
liberation, 46
life and death, 25, 44
ligaments, 47
limitations, x
limited war, 63
linear enemy, 68
locusts, 46
logical ways, 71
long-range plan, 65
long-term adversaries, 68
long-term victory, 18
looming war, 62
Louis-Dreyfus, Julia, 32
luxury in war, 18
Lyme Disease, 49
maggots, 51
main bug character, 27
major military conflict, 39
major military duties, 35
managers, 37
Mandible, General, 17–20, 22
maneuver, 19
mankind, vii, 5–8, 12, 20, 67
marauding soldier-ants, 20
Mars, 6
Marxist gags, 11
massive retaliation, 66
massive weapons, 64
master manipulator, 47
master plan, 24
master warrior, ix, 13
masterpiece on military strategy, 25
matrix of war, ix
May, Rollo, 43
mechanics of war, 73
Mega-tunnel, 24
memorable story, 68
men, 11
mental skills, 60
Messenger, Charles, 1, 3
metaphoric way, 27
Middle East, 4
militaristic, 16
militaries, ix
militaries (of the world), 34
militarily, 67
military, viii, 28, 36, 39
military activity, 37
military advice, 32
military affairs, 16, 33–34
military arm, 72
military body (organ), 35
military build-up, 62, 67, 68
military campaigns and operations, 19
military camps (unpredictable), 60
military combat, 33–34
military conflicts, 72
military confrontations, 72
military considerations, 37

military contrivance, vii
military coup (in U.S.), 36
military culture, 34, 65
military development, 32
military dimensions of conflict, 8
military endeavor, 38
military engineers, 64
military enterprise, 33
military forces, 16, 39
military geniuses, x
military goals, 40
military guile (spontaneous), 60
military historian, 1
military hostilities, 67–68
military implications, 8, 13
military innovations, 73
military judgment, 33
military leaders, ix, 3–4, 8, 13, 17–18, 25, 27, 30, 32, 34–35, 37–40, 68, 72
military-like movement (of soldier ANTZ), 20
military maneuvers, 16
military mind-set, 7
military mission, 39
military operations, 32, 35–37
military opinion, 32–33
military orders, 2, 19
military parochialism, 71
military personnel, 35
military persuasion, 39
military planning, 17, 27
military point of view, 11
military policy, x, 8, 13, 40
military-political implications, 74
military politics, 3, 7, 11
military posture, 60
military pragmatism, 1
military prestige, 59
military service, 1
military soldier, 29
military solutions, 39
military strategists, 3, 27
military strategy, vii, 3, 5, 7–8, 13, 25, 28, 33, 38
military strategy (in war), 72
military strategy objectives, 28
military strength (U.S.), 35
military supremacy, 67
military tactics, 7–8, 25, 31, 53, 73
military tasks (conventional), 36
military technology, 12, 30, 64
military treatises, 9
military war, x
military warriors, 36
military world, 7
Mills, Walter, 27
mind-set, 5
misinterpretation, 69
missiles, 12
mobile launching systems, 64
modern-day battlefield, ix
modern-day battlefield (of humans), 66
modern-day leaders, 74
monolithic, 53, 68
monumental mistake, 54
Moo-Lacka-Moo, 66
Moore, William C. (Major General), 34–35, 38
morbid allegory, 66
mounting a defense, 48
multitude of insects, 57
mutual benefit, 61
Myrer, Anton, 59

nation-states, 31, 38
national defense, ix
national destiny, 66
national dignity, 63
national policy, 28, 39–40
national security, 17
national security objectives, 35
nationalism, 61–62
nations, 68
nature of war, 71
necessary ingredient, 59
neurotic worker ant, 13
New Columbia Encyclopedia, 44
new fangled weapons, 64
new weaponry, 67
New York, vii

no-nonsense soldier, 62
Noble House, 12
non-military duties (activities), 35–36
non-military initiatives (reasons), 36
non-military objectives, 72
non-violent (struggle), 48
nonsensical issues, 67
notions of war, 68
notorious weapons, 66
nuclear arsenals, 31
Nuclear Assured Destruction, 72
nuclear blasts, 47
nuclear conflict, 30
nuclear destructive potential, 68
nuclear nation-state system, 31
nuclear-powered, 12
nuclear strike, 60
nuclear weapons (proliferation), 60
nuclei, 43

object of war, 28
objectives (military) in war, 18, 34
objectives of the military, 31
obliterate ourselves, 73
odd communities, 62
odd devices, 64
On War, 33, 37, 74
one-of-a-kind weapons, 67
operational objectives, 30
opportunity (pursuit of), 34
optimistic, 69
organization, 44
ossify, 47
other-world creatures, 63
outrageous war machinery, 64
overriding concern, 68
overwhelming ant forces, 19
overwhelming destructive potential, 64
overwhelming force, 18

Panettiere, Hayden, 33
paralyzing venom, 49
paramount importance, 5
Paret, Peter, ix, 30, 71
partiality, 74
patriotism, 62
peace, 4, 25, 61, 73–74
peace (true), 68
peace and war, 1, 40
peace-keeping (missions), 35
peacetime, 23, 36
peculiar inhabitants, 65
People's Liberation Army of China, 12
perfect efficiency, 6
pertinent issues, 72
pesticides, 45, 56
petty differences, 74
phenomenon of war, ix
philosopher ant, 48
philosophical differences, 62
plan for war, 6, 49
planet, 45, 56, 74
planet earth, 43
planning for war, 32
plausible explanations, 72
plausible story, 68
poison toxins, 56
poisonous centipede, 49
poisonous secretion, 21
police force, 36
policy, viii
policy in war, 72
policy of appeasement, 68
political alliance, 62
political and social implications, 68
political choice, 67
political creatures, 3
political decision making, 62
political decisions (corrupted), 12, 34, 37, 39
political discourse, 3–4
political feckless purposes, ix
political geography, 12
political ideas, 30
political impact, 27
political intercourse, 17
political jostling, 51
political leaders, 18, 25
political-military concerns, 73

political-military implications of war, 3, 37
political notions, 11
political objectives, 15, 38
political power, ix
political probabilities, 37
political propaganda, 25
political purpose(s), 30, 33, 38
political rationales, 3
political sabotage, 4
political situation, 38
political unit, 3–4
politicians, 33, 37, 72
politics, 2, 12, 72, 73
polluting traffic, 47
Poo-a-Doo Powder, 60
popular culture, vii
possibilities of war, 72
potential devastation, 72
power struggle, 60
powerful rivals, 67
pragmatic, 38
pragmatism, 39, 71
praying Mantis, 48
predator mite, 43
predisposition to make war, 4
president(s), 12–13, 16, 18, 20
prevarication, 73
price of war, 73
primates, 52
prime minister, 12–13, 16, 20
principle of democracy, 40
probability of any war, 74
profane, 61
professional soldier(s), 33
professional warrior bugs, 31
proliferation (dangerous weapons), 63
proliferation (of dooms-day weapons), 68
prophetic story, 60
pseudo-military campaign, 18
pseudo-science, 6
psychological need (deep-seated), 60
psychological-warfare, 50
public opinion, 66
public view, 74
pugnacious Yook (leader), 62
pupae, 51
pure enmity, viii

Queen Mother (ant), 15–16, 23

racial (and cultural) differences, 64
radiation poisoning, 47
raison d´être, 55
rambunctious insects, 49
rambunctious sides, 66
ramifications, 68
Rapoport, Anatol, 33, 36
realities of geography, 73
reflective thinking, 1
religious cult, 66
remarkable trinity, 28
rescue mission, 37
respective (insect) colonies, 8
respective objectives, 67
responsibilities, 71
retaliatory strike (full-scale), 64
revolutionary leader, 15
revolutionary worker, 24
Ricks, Thomas E., 36
rights, 71
risk of death, 37
risk of war, 62
rocket-like projectile vehicles, 64
rules of conduct (in war), 33

Sagan, Carl, 43
Samurai (The Seven), 29
sarin (nerve) gas, 66
scorpions (vicious looking), 48
Scott, George C., 17
secret strategists, 63
Secretary of Defense, 38–39
Secretary of State, 39
self-defeating enterprises, 73
sentience, 7
sentient creatures (insects), 43–44, 55, 57
sentient insects, x, 7, 43

sentimentality, 74
September 11, 2001, 4
Seuss, Dr., ix, x, 59, 68–69
Shinrikyo (Aum), 66
shock wave, 47
Shogun, 12
significant in battle, 66
significant light, 68
similar species, 65
simplistic design, 64
sinister purposes, 64
situational awareness (operations) 35
smart bombs, 12
social (respective) arenas, 12
social organization, 14
society, 73
society of states, 73
soldier ant(s), 14–15, 17–20, 24
soldier ant reserves, 17
soldier ant Weaver, 14
soldier-ANTZ, 20
soldier-termites, 20
soldiers, 13, 16, 35
soldiers of war, 65
Somalia (warlord), 36–37
sophisticated treatise, 12
soul-searching (about war), 73
sovereign nation(s), 16–17, 36
sovereignty, 64–65
sovereignty (individual), 45
Soviet Union, 60, 63, 65–66, 68
Spacey, Kevin, 28
species, 7, 43, 47
spiders, 43
spiders (poisonous), 48
spiritual dimension, 1
splendid termite colony, 20
splendid weapons, 60
Stallone, Sylvester, 14
Star Ship Troopers, 5
state resources, 72
statecraft, 40
statesmanship, 39
statesmen, 28, 34, 38–39
stealth, 50
Stone, Sharon, 14
strange worlds, 65
strategic, 71
strategic military mistakes, 22
strategic practices, 12
strategic questions, 28
strategic warfare, 6
strategy (strategies), ix, 7, 18, 21, 29, 31, 34, 60, 62
strategy in war, 72
Students of Warfare, 1
submarines (nuclear-powered), 12
subways, 66
Sun Tzu, viii, ix, x, 4, 12–14, 16–25, 53, 74
super weapon, 64
supreme being, 43
supreme leader, 16
supreme military leader, 29
surface-to-air-missile, 61
swarm, 50
symbiotic relationship, 15

tactical errors, 22
tactical notions, 31
tactical sense, 59
tactical strategies, 6
tactical system, 64
tactical things, 33
tacticians, viii
tactics, vii, ix, 21
technical advances, 12
technical machinery, 12
technological advancements, 21
technological fire power, 73
technological know-how, 60
technological skills, 35, 55
technologically, 2
technologists, 35
technology (technologies), 2, 34, 40
tense equilibrium, 68
termite enemies, 19
termite fighting force, 21
termite mound(s), 20
termites, 17, 19–21

Termites War, 14, 21
terrible atrocities, 22
terrible military legacy, 61
terrible odds, 18
territorial expansion, 65
territory, 65
terrorism, 4, 30
terrorists, 68
the art of military command, 28
the art of using troops, 20
The Art of War, ix, 11–14, 16–17, 21, 23, 25, 34, 38, 74
The Beginning of a War, 11
The Boys in his Back Room, 63
The Bugs of War, 5, 7
The Butter Battle Book, x, 9, 59–60, 63–64, 66, 68
The Causes of War, 1–2
The Mystery of War, 3
The Role of Civilian Leaders, 32
The Role of Military Leaders, 28
The Soul of Battle, 1
the threat of combat, 72
The War of the Worlds, 6
thermo-nuclear destruction, 64
threat of war, 66
thwart, 60
tit-for-tat, 61
Tokyo, 66
total annihilation, 63
total victory, 18
total war, 27
total war campaign, 22
training for war, 36
transformations of war, 13
Triple-Sling Jigger, 60
Trojan Horse, 7, 32
Troy (city gates), 7
truism, 40
tymbals, 51
tyrannical insect leaders, 8
tyrants, 23, 38

ugly heads, 68
unalterable, 64
unbridled hatred, 15
uncertain terms, 65
unchecked weapons-building, 63
underestimate, 74
understanding the responsibilities, 74
undeterred, 64
unearthly worlds, 64
unification, 62
unilaterally, 62
unintended consequences, 2, 7, 43, 71
unitary, 2
United States, 39, 60, 63–64, 66, 68
unity of purpose, 18, 31
University of Exeter, 66
University of Oxford, viii
unknown territory, 17
unnecessary war, 67
unprecedented secrecy, 62
unpredictable battlefield, 35
unreasonable contempt, 60
unrestrained optimism, 74
unspeakable war, 60
unsuspecting army of termites, 18
unsympathetic, 60
unusual weapons, 64
unwinnable war, 15
use of engagements, 28
utterly sputter, 64

valorize war, 2
Van Itch, 62, 64
varied environments, 12
vengeance, ix
viable alternatives, 40
vicious bug-allies, 29
victimization(and self-loathing), 49
victory in war, 68
Vietnam, 22
villains, 9
violence, 27
violence of humans, 8
violent, 64
violent activities, 74
violent events, ix
violent immolation, xi

violent means, 27
violent war, 66
violently engaging, 67
volatile, 60

Walken, Christopher, 18
war, vii, viii, ix, 1, 4–9, 11, 13–14, 20, 28–30, 33, 35, 36, 38–40, 46–49, 53, 55–57, 60, 63, 66, 68, 71–74
war (impending), 51
war (just and unjust), 8
war (modern), 31
war adventure story, 15
war and peace, 8
war criminal, 23
war-fighters, 37
war fighting, viii, 12–13, 34–35
war-fighting capabilities, 31
war-fighting tactics, 3
war-fighting techniques, 53
war-footing, 60
war hero, 14, 23
war-like, 60, 64
war machine, 19
war machines (terrifying), 64
war of the century, 55
war-plan(s), 52
war room, 63
war-time (situation), 31, 45
war-time attitudes, 5
war-time environment, 65
warfare, x, 8, 28, 35,68, 73
warfare (a theory of), 28
warfare of cartoons, x
warfare strategy, 31
warmongers (cockeyed), 63
warring acumen, 55
warring army of termites, 21
warring insects, 5
warring sides, 64
warrior(s), 23, 34, 36
warrior-ants, 14
warrior-bugs, 28–30
warrior insects, 43
warrior's creed, 7, 37
wars, 2–3, 6–7, 25, 39, 68, 73
wasps, 51
weapons, 13, 64
weapons (during times of war), 16, 31, 47, 61
weapons-building pace, 61
weapons of mass destruction, 64
weapons of war, 12, 47, 59, 63
weapons systems, 35
weird weapons (magnificently), 61
Wells, H.G., 6
West Nile virus, 50
whimsy, 59
white ants, 21
willy-nilly games (of chance), 73
winged-ant (Colonel Cutter), 18
wooden bird, 32
wooden-bird contraption, 33
worker ant, 14
world(s), 43, 52, 60, 63
World Trade Center, vii, 4
World War I, 22
World War II, 22, 66

xenophobic, 61

Yoo, John, 17
Yook commander, 63
Yooks, 59–68
young soldier Yook, 63

Z (worker ant), 13
Zooks, 59–68
Zuckerman, Solly, 63, 68

About the Author

Earnest N. Bracey is a retired Army Lieutenant Colonel, with over twenty years of active military service. He was commissioned through Reserve Officer Training (*Distinguished Military Graduate*) at Jackson State University, where he graduated with honors (*Magna Cum Laude*), and received his bachelor of arts degree in political science in 1974. In addition, he received the Masters of Public Administration in 1979 from Golden Gate University, his Masters of Arts degree in International Affairs in 1983 from the Catholic University of America, and his doctorate of Public Administration (with emphasis in Public Policy) in 1993 from George Mason University. Dr. Bracey also earned his Ph.D. in Education from Capella University in 1999.

A recipient of numerous military awards and civilian honors, he is also a graduate of the United States Naval War College and the Command and General Staff College at Fort Leavenworth, Kansas, and previously served as Director of Administration at the prestigious Industrial College of the Armed Forces, Washington, D.C. He was also recognized as Who's Who Among America's Teachers in 2002, 2003, 2004, 2005, and 2006.

Dr. Bracey is professor of political science, and currently teaches American Politics and Black American History at the Community College of Southern Nevada in Las Vegas. He was formerly Chair and Professor of Political Science Department at Jackson State University and Chairperson of Political Science and History Department at Hampton University. He serves as an editorial board-member for the Nevada Historical Society Quarterly. His work has appeared in professional journals and other publications, and he is the author of the books, *Prophetic Insights: The Higher Education and Pedagogy of African Americans*, University Press of America, 1999, *On Racism: Essays On Black Popular Culture, African American Politics, and the New Black*

Aesthetics, University Press of America, 2003, *Daniel "Chappie" James: The First African American Four Star General*, McFarland & Company, Inc., 2003, and *Places in Political Time: Voices From the Black Diaspora*, 2005. He also co-authored the book, *American Politics and Culture Wars* (2001). He is also the author of the novels, *Choson* (1994) and *The Black Samurai* (1998), and the book of short stories, *Requiems for Black Folks*, 2002.

www.ingramcontent.com/pod-product-compliance
Lightning Source LLC
Chambersburg PA
CBHW021834300426
44114CB00009BA/441
9780761835387